Great Producers

Visionaries of the American Theater

Iris Dorbian

ALLWORTH PRESS
NEW YORK

12 11 10 09 08   5 4 3 2 1

Published by Allworth Press
An imprint of Allworth Communications, Inc.
10 East 23rd Street, New York, NY 10010

Cover design by Derek Bacchus
Interior design by Kristina Critchlow
Page composition/typography by Integra Software Services, Pvt., Ltd.,
Puducherry, India
Cover photo by Derrek Bacchus

ISBN-13: 978-1-58115-646-1
ISBN-10: 1-58115-646-4

Library of Congress Cataloging-in-Publication Data:
Dorbian, Iris.
  Great producers : visionaries of the American theater / Iris Dorbian.
    p. cm.
  Includes bibliographical references and index.
  ISBN-13: 978-1-58115-646-1
  ISBN-10: 1-58115-646-4
1. Theatrical producers and directors—United States—Biography. I. Title.

PN2285.D66 2008
792.02'320922—dc22

                                                        2008010969
Printed in the United States of America

Dedicated to the memory of David Brian Baker and Nathalie Ackerman.

TABLE OF CONTENTS

Acknowledgements

It may sound like a tired maxim, but there are very few things in life that are a solo effort. The assistance and generosity accorded to me throughout the process of writing this book clearly illustrates that. I humbly and graciously thank the following individuals for making my life so much easier by taking the time to speak to me to offer their much-valued musings on various producers: Nils Hanson, Doris Eaton Travis, John Kenrick, Gillian Lynne, Jack O'Brien, Adam Epstein, Roger Horchow, Susan Dietz, Ted Snowdon, Debra Monk, Charles Busch, Bartlett Sher, Bob Crowley, Natasha Katz, John Rando, William Ivey Long, Walter Bobbie, Allison Harper, and Wanda Richert.

Also, a special round of applause must be extended to Michael Kantor for pointing me toward Doris Eaton Travis, the centenarian survivor of the *Ziegfeld Follies*, and Ken Billington for his kindness in sending me excerpts of Louis Hartmann's *Stage Lighting*.

Many kudos go to überpublicists Susanne Tighe, Julianna Hannett, Aaron Meier, and Barbara Carroll for their logistical expertise in helping to coordinate interviews. Thank you from the bottom of my heart.

And lastly, a rousing encore to the assistants of the producers—Greg Roby, Brett England, Clark Tedesco, Dusty Bennett, and Lily Hung—all of whom were studies in meticulous detail and fluid cooperation.

Thank you all!

Introduction

When I interviewed Walter Bobbie, the gifted performer turned Tony Award–winning director of the 1996 Broadway revival *Chicago,* about his experiences working with Fran Weissler, one of the producers profiled on the ensuing pages, I asked him point-blank what makes a good producer. (This was a ubiquitous question that I posed to nearly everyone I interviewed for the book—both producers and the people they work with, which include coproducers, designers, directors, and actors.) His response was so passionately forthright and hauntingly eloquent, I knew once I transcribed his interview onto my laptop that it was going to be a quote I would use to preface my book:

> Courage. The thing that a producer has to know, well, before anyone else says it, before the awards come, before the critics say yes, is that he believes so much in this creative expression that he's willing to bank his money and reputation in vigorous support of this. That takes confidence and courage.

I believe all the producers I discuss in this book, from the rising young general manager/producer Roy Gabay to the elegant former Wall Street wizard Roger Berlind, have both confidence and courage in spades. As many told me in interviews conducted between October 2006 and August 2007, they've all had to invoke these qualities when taking on decidedly less than commercial projects. Whether it was erstwhile theater critic/dramaturg Jack Viertel, teaming up with Margo Lion to produce Tony Kushner's *Angels in America: Millennium Approaches* and *Perestroika,* or Barry and Fran Weissler tackling William Finn's *Falsettos* and encountering one roadblock after another, these producers have all displayed remarkable daring in the face of adversity, sticking tenaciously to their convictions even when common sense, reflected in declining box-office sales and middling reviews, dictated otherwise.

The book is not intended to be a legal primer on how to produce. For that, I urge you to flip to the appendix and check out the suggested volumes in the Books section. Nor is this book tailored to be a no-holds-barred, sensationalistic look at the sordid backstage machinations of producing. For that, you're better off logging onto one of the many theater gossip blogs that pop up regularly on the Internet. Yes, there is plenty of good dish in this book, but not on the tier of gossip you would normally find in a book whose sole intent is to titillate readers with lurid personal tidbits. (The exception is the rascally David Merrick, who seems to have been cast in a mold unlike anyone else before or since.) The "dirt" that you will glean from this book is how these producers got started, what project their initial foray into producing was, what their most challenging project was, how they deal with the irksome task of soliciting money from prospective donors, how they deal with a show that flops, etc. All are matters that every producer worth his or her salt, whether he or she is working on Broadway, off-Broadway, on tours or in regional theater, has had to grapple with sometime in his or her career. For the sake of expediency, simply because there were so many producers to discuss, I narrowed my focus to Broadway commercial and nonprofit producers.

When I began working on this book, my aim was to offer a behind-the-scenes peek into how each producer approaches his or her craft. Certain things seem to be a consensus: producing is impossibly risky—or "a silly thing," as Michael David, crusty president of Dodger Theatricals, refers to it—and asking people for money is never an easy chore. But the major common denominator is how proactive all of these producers are. They're not just moneylenders, and if they were, they wouldn't be in this book. All are actively involved in all phases of their shows, from beginning stages to opening night to closing. They are not perfect, and many do own up to mistakes they've made while producing certain projects, but unlike others, they've learned from their errors and have leveraged their hard-won wisdom into bigger and better shows. Therein lies the secret to their greatness. For students, educators, and aspiring producers, you couldn't ask for more worthwhile models for inspiration and edification.

As you will gather when you read each chapter, the modern producers are a divergent lot, and not in the mold of their predecessors: Flo Ziegfeld, David Belasco, David Merrick, and Joseph Papp. These men defined the older archetype of what a producer used to be: larger than life, irascible, despotic, and morally flawed (although Papp's genuine altruism, crusading fever, and championship of the rank and file countervails his micromanaging propensities).

Nowadays, the theater producer is a far different species. Not only do producers frequently collaborate with one another (Broadway producing circles are quite incestuous—note the repeated references to the same shows and producers made by those interviewed in this book), but it's rare indeed that one can operate independently à la Merrick: the harsh economics of producing on Broadway forbid that. Whatever the modern prolific theater producers may lack in color, charisma, and sheer brashness, they certainly make up for in business acumen, creative audacity, and utter resilience. This book is an homage to their innate derring-do and the everlasting pursuit of their next project.

Iris Dorbian
New York City
August 2007

SECTION I
The Impresario

CHAPTER 1
Florenz Ziegfeld

b. March 21, 1867, Chicago, IL, USA – **d.** July 22, 1932, Hollywood, CA, USA

"To create the Follies and thereby make revues, a Broadway institution was impressive enough, but this man also had the nerve to produce Show Boat. No wonder he remains the greatest musical producer Broadway has ever known."

—John Kenrick, NYU and Marymount College professor of musical theater history/author of Musicals101.com

Florenz Ziegfeld

Spare No Expense

He was a womanizer and a gambler; a shameless publicity-hound and a demanding perfectionist. The former qualities probably did not serve him well as a steady beau or husband in his various relationships, but the latter attributes made him an impresario extraordinaire. (According to legend, Ziegfeld even had calling cards created with that title!) There was never an incident too bizarre or too mundane for the cunning Chicago native to exploit for promotional purposes. Whether it was claiming that Anna Held, his top talent (and then squeeze) had saved someone's life after falling from a bicycle, or that a glass bowl filled with nothing but water contained invisible fish (a ruse he tried as a child), Ziegfeld shrewdly parlayed the power of hype—and audacity— into a several-decades-long career that would eventually sputter to its demise with the 1929 Wall Street crash. With his entire fortune—three million dollars, then a titanic amount—obliterated, Ziegfeld bravely tried to forge on, staging another version of his legendary *Follies,* a show featuring a Rodgers and Hart score, and yet another production of *Show Boat,* but it was to little avail. Beset by mountainous debts (which his last wife, the actress Billie Burke, had diligently tried to pay off by accepting one film role after another), Ziegfeld died of pleurisy on July 22, 1932. And yet despite the downward spiral of his final years, his name is synonymous with "showman par excellence."

Quality over Quantity

Sheer gumption is not enough to catapult a producer into the rarefied realm of greatness, and Ziegfeld was no dilettante. He spared no expense when it came to acquiring the finest talent money could offer. Fanny Brice, W. C. Fields, Will Rogers, Eddie Cantor, Lillian Lorraine, and Marilyn Miller were among the many talents Ziegfeld turned into stars when they joined his fabled *Follies.* He also shelled out enormous money for costumes, never deigning to use anything synthetic.

"If something was supposed to be silk, then they'd use real silk and go to Europe to get it," says Nils Hanson, administrator of the Ziegfeld Club, a New York City–based archive devoted to the master producer. "He [was extravagant] and obviously, for that reason, he went broke many times over."

His insatiable appetite for gambling didn't help either, although according to Hanson, "he was fortunate that his first wife Anna Held did help him out to some degree" until temptress Lillian Lorraine sashayed in ("she got away with murder because of her beauty") and the Held/Ziegfeld union disintegrated. "When Lorraine wouldn't marry him, he married Billie Burke in 1913. That marriage lasted."

From *Ziegfeld Follies* (1926), featuring Marion Benda (center)

He also adhered to an exhausting schedule that would break the backs of most workaholics. But he was obsessed and he had a vision—and from that emanated the source of his brilliance.

Becoming a Folly

Doris Eaton Travis, 102, has spent much of her life in show business; she got her start in the *Ziegfeld Follies* at age fourteen after tagging along to see her sister Pearl, who was in charge of training dancers for the tours, in rehearsal. The *Follies* choreographer, Ned Wayburn, noticed the teen-age Doris as well as her startling resemblance to his wife; he asked Pearl whether her kid sister could dance. Pearl said yes, since Doris had been performing since she was six.

"He said, 'I'm looking for someone to understudy Ann Pennington (a Ziegfeld headliner) on the road—could she do Ann Pennington's routines?' Pearl said, 'Oh yes, she can,' because she knew I could do them. So Mr. Wayburn said, 'I'd like to have her go on the road and understudy Ann Pennington.' So Pearl said, 'I don't know if that's possible, Mr. Wayburn. She's only fourteen and I don't think our mother would let her go.' He then said, 'Would you go tell your mother she can travel with her? I can pay her expenses, but I want Doris to go on the road and understudy Ann

Pennington.' We went home, talked it over, and it was agreed that I would do that. That was my start with the *Ziegfeld Follies.*" It was 1918 and Travis would go on to dance with three editions of the *Follies.*

Travis, who later began a successful string of Arthur Murray dance studios in Michigan and had a local talk show, prizes her past association with Ziegfeld, especially in light of the fact that she and several of her siblings— sister Mary, younger brother Charlie, and the aforementioned Pearl—had performed in the *Follies* at one time.

"It was always a wonderful asset to say I was in the *Ziegfeld Follies,*" says Travis. She lauds his commitment to having "great quality in [Florenz Ziegfeld's] productions. His comedians were not the rough type at all. They were very classy comedians—Eddie Cantor and W. C. Fields. And Will Rogers was one of the top performers, and Marilyn Miller. The members of the show were always very capable dancers."

Lover of Beauty

Hanson echoes Travis' belief that Ziegfeld's drive to incorporate the finest per formers and production elements in his shows factored greatly in his success. He also feels Ziegfeld's showcasing of the supple female form, coupled with the most dazzling visuals, set a standard in the American theater.

"He concentrated on beauty and glamour and exotic settings. This was the first producer that did that, and all those that followed seem to copy him, right up to present-day Las Vegas," he says. Modern showgirls definitely have their genesis in the prototype first put forth by Ziegfeld. Any time you see a promotional photo of a beautiful, voluptuous girl advertising a revue, you might just have to doff your hat in silent reverence to Ziegfeld.

In the Beginning

Born in Chicago on either March 15 or 21, 1857, Ziegfeld's future calling would come as a result of another's misfortune—in this case, his German-born father, whose nightclub, the Trocadero, was seriously floundering. The club, which had opened its doors in anticipation of the hubbub expected to ensue around the impending World's Fair in Chicago, had booked a menu of classi cal music and variety acts that was as enticing to the local throngs as heat is to Eskimos. Young Flo stepped in to act as his family's savior. He found Eugene Sandow, a muscled Charles Atlas of his day, and booked him in the Trocadero. With each gleaming bicep and deltoid Sandow flexed and bared to swoon ing ladies, the Ziegfeld family took one step away from the brink of ruin—all thanks to their budding impresario. Ziegfeld would tour with Sandow, becom ing a great success before opting for the footlights of ole Broadway.

In 1907, Ziegfeld began the first of his seminal stage extravaganzas, the *Follies* (inspired by the *Folies Bergère* in Paris), which would showcase leggy beauties while featuring scores by composers along the luminous lines of Jerome Kern, Irving Berlin, and George Gershwin. Ziegfeld got financing from theater owners Abe Erlanger and Marc Klaw, who were looking for an act that would take the wind out of the sails of their rivals, the Shubert brothers, who were experiencing a flush of success with a string of revues at the Hippodrome Theatre. The *Follies* opened in the roof garden venue of the New York Theatre. Erlanger dubbed it the *Jardin de Paris*. In spite of the fancy moniker, the ambience was shabby—although it did afford audiences exposure to a balmy summer breeze, in an era where air-conditioning was only a pipe dream. In 1913, the *Follies* would move into Erlanger and Klaw's New Amsterdam Theatre on 42nd Street.

The *Follies* became a smash sensation, and when Ziegfeld brought it on its first tour, the production netted a then whopping $130,000 at the box office. Considering the total production cost was $13,800, the tour had recouped its investment and then some. Ziegfeld was soon planning a new version of *Follies*. Though he would produce other shows, the *Follies* always remained his top priority.

A true iconoclast, Ziegfeld broke the racial code by hiring Bert Williams, a top vaudevillian who was the first black man to perform with white artists

From *Ziegfeld Midnight Frolic*

on a Broadway stage. Though Ziegfeld withstood a storm of public indignation over this act, he steadfastly refused to be swayed by prejudice.

Throughout this period, Ziegfeld continued to fan publicity by planting goofy news items about his stars. For instance, although Fanny Brice had been a respected comedienne/singer on the burlesque circuit when he hired her, Ziegfeld claimed that he had discovered her as a street urchin selling newspapers underneath the Brooklyn Bridge. The public didn't believe this fabrication, but Brice knew the inherent value of publicity and wasn't about to refute the canard either.

The End Is Near—or Is It?

The 1927 debut of the first "talkie" movie, *The Jazz Singer,* would spell the onset of the end for Ziegfeld. The lavish production values that had been de rigueur for a Ziegfeld show were also standard for talkies. Soon the audiences that had once flocked in droves to the New Amsterdam Theatre were clamoring like mad to get in to see the latest talkie. Sadly, Ziegfeld was becoming a relic of a bygone age. It was over and he knew it. Though he would achieve success in the latter part of his life with his production of Jerome Kern/Oscar Hammerstein's *Show Boat,* a musical adaptation of Edna Ferber's 1926 book that touched upon miscegenation among performers on a Mississippi showboat in the late 19th century, Ziegfeld's end loomed near. The great irony here is that *Show Boat,* which Ziegfeld produced on his own, is widely considered to be a milestone in the history of the Broadway musical because it's the first book musical. Prior to *Show Boat,* musicals were simply revues; after its creation, the art form would incorporate a narrative that had three vital dramatic components: a beginning, a middle, and an end. *Show Boat* set the bar that would later be met—and surpassed—by subsequent musical theater greats, such as Rodgers and Hammerstein or Stephen Sondheim. *Show Boat,* which premiered on Broadway at the Ziegfeld Theatre (the consummate showman had spent $2.5 million building it) on December 27, 1927, where it ran for a year and a half, is perhaps Ziegfeld's greatest legacy, simply because it has lived on in subsequent productions, whereas the *Follies* exist only in photo archives—and for others like Travis—in memory.

Plagued by debts, lawsuits stemming from unpaid bills, an omnipresent fear of death, ailing health, and financial ruin, the master showman bravely continued on. He would stage shows, adhering to his old production model, but because of the Depression and because his style was no longer fashionable, audiences were not forthcoming.

"He was a dreamer, a supplier of fantasies. He was not even in the usual sense a human being, but a strange monster who breathed fire into a moribund vaudeville and into the duller and more phlegmatic spirits of his contemporaries," writes Charles Higham in his 1972 biography *Ziegfeld*. "He revolutionized at every level: in the use of color in costumes and sets, in the blending of music with action, in the reduction of long comedy acts to sketches integrated with a whole work, in destroying the very word 'vulgarity' in relation to the American stage.... He was a giant and he remains one. If in the last analysis he seems impossibly remote, it is because we cannot see quite that high."

When asked what Ziegfeld's contributions are to the American theater, Doris Eaton Travis, the centenarian who knew him firsthand, succinctly answers, "Quality, beauty, refinement; everything that was lovely and that a theater should present in a musical show."

Career Highlights

- Mastermind behind the *Ziegfeld Follies*
- Introduced Fanny Brice to audiences in the *Ziegfeld Follies* which she would headline from 1910 to the 1930s; in the 1921 Follies, her song "My Man" became her signature hit
- In 1910, he broke the color-casting barrier in the *Follies* with Bert Williams, an African-American performer.
- In addition to Brice, cast Eddie Cantor in *Whoopee* (1928) and employed the Gershwin brothers for *Rosalie* (1928); George Gershwin composed the music with Sigmund Romberg while Ira wrote the lyrics with P. G. Wodehouse.
- Spent $2.5 million building his namesake theater, the Ziegfeld, which opened in February 1927 with his production of *Rio Rita*
- Produced the first book musical, *Show Boat,* a milestone in American musical theater; the show opened on December 27, 1927 at the Ziegfeld and closed on May 4, 1929.

CHAPTER 2
David Belasco

b. July 25, 1853, San Francisco, CA, USA – **d.** May 14, 1931, New York, NY, USA

"Belasco was the first director/producer who spent weeks lighting his shows and had his electrician invent lighting equipment."

—Tony Award–winning lighting designer Ken Billington

David Belasco dressed in his trademark priestly garb

Unsung Technical Innovator

In his lifetime, Belasco wrote more than one hundred plays that were produced for the Broadway stage. He was also an actor, stage manager, theater owner, and, of course, a producer. He made his stage debut playing Emperor Norton in the play *The Gold Demon* and, because of this role, was subsequently nicknamed "Governor" and the "Bishop of Broadway." As a teen, he got his start at a San Francisco theater as a play adapter and "call boy." From there the seeds were sown for one of American theater's most remarkable careers. And yet in the last chapter of his life, Belasco was dismissed as passé, a ludicrous relic of the past—very much like Ziegfeld. This rejection was ascribed to Belasco's dependence on melodrama in his stage productions thanks to an early association with Dion Boucicault, the legendary playwright who specialized in this overwrought genre. Belasco was a secretary to Boucicault, and supposedly it was Boucicault who encouraged the young Belasco to try his hand at playwriting. After realism progenitors such as Ibsen, Strindberg, Shaw, and Zola entered the scene, Belasco, realizing he was behind the times, introduced naturalism into his shows—except he went overboard, as was his natural wont. He recreated laundromats onstage, restaurants, kitchens—three-dimensional scenic pictures with palpable, tactile detail. Despite this, his dramas still bore heavy vestiges of melodrama.

Into the Light

Yet on closer examination, perhaps it was Belasco's stellar reputation that was the problem with the young up-and-coming Turks. In order to build their own public esteem, they had to lower his. For there remains very little doubt that he was one of the first in modern theater to pioneer realism in stage productions, revolutionizing everything from lighting and scenic design to performance.

Perhaps one of his greatest achievements—and legacies—is his groundbreaking use of lighting. Belasco eliminated the need for footlights by concentrating on follow spots and naturalistic stage illumination. Working with his head electrician, Louis Hartmann (who would later write a book about his collaborations with the versatile producer called *Theatre Lighting*), and future lighting inventors John H. and Anton Kliegl, Belasco incorporated in his inventory equipment that was cutting-edge and state-of-the-art. Color was key to his lighting palette because it set up a mood, an atmosphere. He even used myriad lighting hues that would mesh well with his actors' complexions, whether they were onstage or in their dressing rooms.

As Hartmann writes in his 1930 book, the lighting was not only a top priority for Belasco, but as important as the performances: "It took some time to light any sort of a scene, but detail work consumed the major portion of it, and hours would slip by while we experimented on some effect that appeared simple enough after we had perfected it. Mr. Belasco would generally begin before bringing the players on the stage by getting the scene lighted. The lights were graduated and balanced so the setting had the proper effect for the time of the action.... [Belasco] would spend hours obtaining some seemingly infinitesimal result on which other producers would not waste five minutes."

The Prime of His Life

In his heyday, Belasco owned two theaters: the Republic, which he had leased from Oscar Hammerstein (grandfather of the great lyricist), and the Stuyvesant, which he had built in 1907 for the then princely sum of $750,000. The Stuyvesant, now called the Belasco, continues as a Broadway house (owned by the Shubert Organization) to this day. (In a confusing turn of events, the Republic was originally named the Belasco until 1910, when the Stuyvesant was renamed the Belasco; meanwhile, the Belasco reverted to its original appellation, the Republic.) Like Ziegfeld, Belasco was a lover of luxury, evidenced by his namesake theater's ornate décor. He also kept offices and an opulent apartment for himself in a penthouse he added in the Belasco Theater two years after it opened.

Belasco's mystique is such that he inspired several myths around himself. Theater lore has it that Belasco gave Mary Pickford, one of his many players before she hit it big in Hollywood, her stage name. There are also rumors that the "casting couch" procedure might have started with him (though Belasco was married to Cecelia Loverich for over fifty years, siring two daughters with her). But the strangest and most intriguing of the myths is that of a ghost—supposedly Belasco's—which periodically haunts the balcony of his theater, especially when the show playing onstage is a hit. In Heather Cross's list of locations that are haunted by ghosts, posted on About.com's guide to New York City, the Belasco ghost sightings are prominently placed at the top of the list.

"Numerous accounts of hauntings at one of New York City's oldest the-aters include sightings of the building's builder and namesake, David Belasco, who lived in an apartment at the top of the theater before his death in 1931. His ghost is said to interact with actors, offering kudos and handshakes, and many have reported hearing footsteps and the disconnected elevator running. Sightings of the Blue Lady, possibly Belasco's companion, have been reported numerous times." (On a recent trip to the Belasco Theatre to see a revival of

Clifford Odets's *Awake and Sing,* I asked an usher about this. She responded with great animation, wildly gesticulating about how she's heard this to be true—although she never saw Belasco's apparition materialize in front of her.)

Tyrant or Perfectionist?

Being a producer was central to Belasco's psyche because it reinforced his control over his actors, staff, and production. Not only did he exercise his sovereignty by the fact that he owned the theaters his actors performed in, wrote the plays he cast them in, and then directed the productions they performed in, but he further asserted his power by employing manipulative behavior. One account has him throwing rehearsed temper tantrums that would consist of him stomping on an expensive-looking pocket watch and then storming out, to the horror of his cast. But don't weep over Belasco's violent waste of an extravagant timepiece: Supposedly he had dozens of similar pocket watches carefully hidden in his office.

When he wasn't staging faux tantrums, Belasco was an exacting taskmaster and a perfectionist. He would cast then unknown actors, such as Blanche Bates, Frances Starr, and David Warfield, in roles suitable to their temperaments and types, and rehearse them for ten weeks before setting the show onstage. This is in stark contrast to the general routine nowadays of rehearsing actors for three to four weeks before opening the show.

The Road to the Rialto

Belasco's journey to Broadway came by way of Gustave Frohman, who brought him to New York in 1882 to work as a stage manager and play-wright for the Madison Square Theatre. Two years later, Belasco got a job performing similar duties at Daniel Frohman's Lyceum Theatre (Daniel Frohman was Gustave's brother), where he would remain until 1890. (At the Lyceum, Belasco was a teacher in the theatre's acting school, which later became the blueprint for the American Academy of Dramatic Arts.) He then became an independent producer, where he was involved in writing and directing dozens of productions.

During this turning point in his career, Belasco was evolving into "America's foremost exponent of a theatrical style in which all the individual elements of a production, from text to setting, props, lighting, and acting, operate as completely integrated parts subordinate to the larger, realistic whole," writes Lisa-Lone Marker in her 1974 book *David Belasco: Naturalism in the American Theatre.* Offering a penetrating, if turgid, reappraisal of the unheralded legend's creative output, Marker further notes that Belasco "represented a unique quality in the theater because he combined a thorough, practical knowledge of acting with experience as a director, a producer, and a playwright. His mind grasped all phases of a production and he visualized it as a totality."

With his first play, *May Blossom* (1884), a romantic Civil War melodrama about a man who discovers his friend has betrayed him by marrying his sweetheart (when he wanted his friend to tell her that he had been arrested as a spy and had not deserted her), Belasco fared well in his early collaborations with fellow dramatist Henry C. DeMille. The most prominent example of their dual effort was *The Wife* (1887), a comedy about a woman who marries a man on the rebound. Throughout this time, Belasco was writing plays to be booked by the Theatrical Syndicate—a relationship that ended in 1902 over a clash about money. Created in 1886 by a consortium of producers and investors that included Frohman, Abe Erlanger, and Marc Klaw, the Theatrical Syndicate exerted an unhealthy dominion on the American theater with its monopolizing of contracts and bookings until the late 1910s, when it was finally shattered by the Shuberts.

From 1902 to 1915, Belasco vaulted to the pinnacle of his professional life. Not only would he control two theaters, but he would stage over forty original productions and revivals at his theaters and on tour. Among his plays that reigned supreme were *The Easiest Way* (1909) and *The Governor's Lady* (1912). The great composer Puccini adapted two of Belasco's plays, *Madame Butterfly* (1900) and *The Girl of the Golden West* (1905), into operas respectively.

Forgotten Master

The Belasco Theatre notwithstanding, Belasco's legacy is—sadly—largely forgotten, though theater scholars do credit him with being the first producer to innovate special effects onstage. However, if there was ever a producer who defined the notion of the Renaissance Man, it was this larger-than-life colorful character of Sephardic Jewish heritage, who was given to wearing black clothes and a priestly collar. In 1919, Belasco's memoir, *The Theatre Through Its Stage Door*, was released. Published by Harper & Brothers, the book contained advice to aspiring actors as well as information about the rehearsal process and working with child actors.

The curtain finally fell on Belasco in 1931. Among his last productions were *It's a Wise Child*, which starred future celluloid tough guy Humphrey Bogart, and *Tonight or Never*, starring onstage and offstage acting couple Melvyn Douglas and Helen Gahagan.

At the time of Belasco's passing, the artistic climate of the country had been irrevocably altered by the Depression and by motion pictures with sound; it would be another decade before the nation would be swept into the vortex of World War II. The creative milieu that had spawned and nurtured Belasco was no more.

"His theater was one of fundamental consistency, firmly bound by a single style and thus acquiring its own truth, its own peculiar meaning and poignancy," muses Lisa-Lone Marker. "Herein lies the source of its great success in its own time as well as the seeds, once the tastes and ideals of that time had altered, of its subsequent decline."

Career Highlights

- Discovered silent-screen star Mary Pickford
- Cast Humphrey Bogart in one of his plays prior to his Hollywood career
- Introduced naturalistic stage lighting and scenic design
- Owned two theaters in his heyday: The first Belasco Theater, which he took over in 1902 and gave up in 1910; and the second one, which was built as the Stuyvesant Theatre in 1907 and renamed after Belasco in 1910. The theater continues on as a Broadway venue to this day.
- Wrote and directed many of his shows
- First produced play was *May Blossom* (1884)
- Wrote over forty plays in his lifetime

CHAPTER 3
David Merrick

b. November 27, 1911, St. Louis, MO, USA – **d.** April 25, 2000, London, ENGLAND

"With theater there is knowledge, but more important than knowledge, it's instinct; it's massive instinct, and if you haven't gotten that, it's bad. Merrick had it in spades."

—Gillian Lynne, director/choreographer

"There will never be another David Merrick."

—Wanda Richert, star of *42nd Street*

David Merrick.

The Firebrand
In 1966, he made the cover of the March 25 issue of *Time* magazine as
"Broadway's David Merrick," alongside a drawing of his formidable self in
profile, with his trademark moustache, bulging eyes—and lengthy list of
credits. Such a lofty acknowledgment was no surprise, since all throughout
the 1950s and 1960s, Merrick was *the* archetypal producer. The singular
embodiment of success—and ruthlessness—in the American theater, the
St. Louis native had an uncanny ability for picking hits and producing dozens
of shows in a period when Broadway was on a decline. With his law-school
trained verbal adroitness (which he used to withering effect on his enemies
and those who would challenge him) and unbridled ambition, Merrick sub-
limated the insecurities of his youth. The only present-day counterpart to his
high-profile career may be that of Cameron Mackintosh, a man of decidedly
different temperament but equal ardor for theater.

Growing Up
It was this love, this unquenchable fervor, that would be the sole sustenance
for Merrick during the last chapter of his life, after he suffered a disabling
stroke in 1983 that left this fiercely proud, vigorous man unable to speak and
his once sharp-as-a-tack mind blurry and confused. Theater and theater alone
was his panacea, his magical elixir.

"It had always been true," wrote the *New York Daily News* theater critic
Howard Kissel in his unflattering but comprehensively detailed 1993 book,
David Merrick: The Abominable Showman: The Unauthorized Biography. "The
theater had always mobilized [Merrick's] energies and cleared his mind. It
had always been the force that turned him from a soft, unprepossessing figure
on the periphery to the powerful, mesmerizing tyrant who controlled others'
lives. The theater gave him control of his life."

Born November 27, 1911, in St. Louis, Missouri, David Merrick, née
Margulois, was the son of Sam, whom Kissel describes as a "hapless provider,"
and the mentally unstable Celia. Like some other children of Russian and
Eastern European Jewry who had parents who spoke with thick accents,
Merrick grew up ashamed of his origins and often tried to distance himself
from it by either not owning up to his heritage or telling friends he was "half
Jewish." Remember, this was the early part of the 20th century, when anti-
Semitism was barely concealed, even in so-called metropolitan hubs. Being
overtly Jewish was—tragically—not a route to success but ghettoization.
Assimilation was considered the only answer, which is why many Jews like
Merrick wishing to gain entrée into a rarefied segment of society that would
have otherwise ostracized them for their ethnicities changed their surnames
and created identities separate from their background.

In addition to dealing with discrimination, Merrick had to struggle with a chaotic family life. When he was ten years old, his parents divorced for a second time (they had divorced when he was seven but reconciled afterward, only to realize that the reconciliation was a mistake). Thus began a very turbulent phase in his life; Merrick's determination to succeed might have had its genesis during this beleaguered period. Merrick was the youngest child in the family; his older siblings were all out of the house by the time of the second divorce. His unbalanced mother would soon be committed to a mental institution and Merrick would start being shuttled from one sister to another. Supposedly he overheard one of the sisters complain to another about having him for "six months in the spring—now it's your turn."[1]

According to Kissel, the only ray of light during this sad period was from his brother-in-law Maurice, the husband to Etta, one of his sisters. Maurice loved the theater and used all his spare time to direct amateur shows at the St. Louis branch of the YMHA. For the first time in a life defined by inattention and abandonment, young Merrick found something that enlivened and validated his existence: theater.

Soon his idol would be Florenz Ziegfeld, and like that consummate showman, Merrick entertained ambitions about becoming a producer. He was interested in staging similar theatrical spectacles teeming with statuesque beauties, elaborate sets and costumes—visual feasts for the senses. In the meantime, he got a BA and later a law degree from St. Louis University.

New York, New York

Feeling he needed to be in New York City to fulfill his mushrooming dreams, Merrick took his new wife, Lenore, a local girl with a sizable inheritance, and made his move in 1940. Through the referral of a friend, Merrick (who had changed his name legally at this juncture) began working as an office assistant for producer Herman Shumlin. This turned out to be an auspicious apprenticeship because it would teach Merrick a great deal about commercial theater and producing. Nearly ten years after his arrival in Gotham, Merrick would finally (with the aid of various partners) produce a play entitled *Clutterbuck* by Benn Levy, about romantic entanglements aboard a Caribbean cruise; it opened on Broadway in December 1949 and ran for 218 performances. The initial investment was $50,000, $5,000 of which Merrick put in.

Merrick's predilection for self-promotion, another integral part of his success, would be fully exemplified by his advertising campaigns for *Clutterbuck*. Because the reviews were lukewarm at best, Merrick needed ways to entice theatergoers to see the show. He submitted ads to newspapers, full of risqué double entendres; he even included doggerels that were admittedly silly, such as, "We make no claim that he's a saint. As a matter of fact we insist he ain't—CLUTTERBUCK!" *Clutterbuck* was soon included in the *Best Plays of 1949–50*, a prestigious anthology that also had in this volume William Inge's *Come Back Little Sheba* and Carson McCullers's *The Member of the Wedding*.

His next show, though, would be critical for Merrick, one that would cause him to later remark that he was truly born when the production opened. The show was *Fanny*, a musical adaptation of a film by Marcel Parcel Pagnol (*Fanny* was part of a trilogy along with *Marius* and *Caesar*). Merrick became obsessed with producing *Fanny*, and to seal the deal, he flew to France to meet with the elderly, ailing Pagnol to get the rights. After much begging, the old man, impressed with the younger man's wherewithal and drive, yielded.

Next Merrick needed to find a director for *Fanny*. There was one he already had his eye on—Joshua Logan, famed director of such stage classics as *South Pacific* and *Picnic*. Through the noted set designer Jo Mielziner (who met Merrick via Edward Kook of the Century Lighting Company), Merrick was introduced to Logan; he then screened Pagnol's film *Marius* for him.

Neither the film nor Merrick made a strong impression on Logan. But a year later, after Merrick went through a succession of book writers for the tuner, the budding producer invited Logan back for another screening of a Pagnol film. Finally, Logan was swayed. He couldn't wait to direct the project.

On November 4, 1954, *Fanny* opened at the Majestic Theater, where it ran for 888 performances. Like *Clutterbuck*, *Fanny* garnered middling reviews; ticket sales were hardly climbing (although Merrick did raise prices to the then unprecedented sum of $7.50 apiece, which he deemed necessary for promotion and to insure that his backers—all sixty-five of them—would get a quick return for their investment).

If New Yorkers thought they were exposed to Merrick, the master of self-promotion and publicity stunts with *Clutterbuck*'s ribald ads, they hadn't seen anything yet. Merrick commissioned a sculpture of Nejla Ates, the belly dancer who appeared in *Fanny*, to be placed in Central Park. He also took out full-page ads in major newspapers like the *New York Times* and the *Tribune*, as well as in foreign papers and even on ocean liners, targeting tourists interested in visiting New York City.

And that was not all. He put up a billboard advertising the show in Penn Station, where commuters would see it every day, and ran ads for *Fanny* in over forty American cities. In addition, the cast appeared on "The Ed Sullivan Show," a very popular television variety program, performing scenes from the show. For Merrick's efforts, *Fanny* would net a profit of nearly a million dollars, a very pretty penny in those days.

A Legend Is Born

Fanny was the harbinger of many more shows that would reinforce and solidify the ongoing Merrick legend. They would include *Gypsy* (with book by Arthur Laurents, music by Jule Styne, and lyrics by Stephen Sondheim), *Irma La Douce, Hello, Dolly!* (with music and lyrics by Jerry Herman and book by Michael Stewart), *I Do! I Do!* (with book, lyrics, and music by Tom Jones and Harvey Schmidt), and *Promises, Promises* (with book by Neil Simon, music by Burt Bacharach, and lyrics by Hal David). Merrick would also import the finest of talent from across the pond by introducing John Osborne, Tom Stoppard, and other great British playwrights to American audiences. Shows such as *Look Back in Anger, The Entertainer,* and *A Taste of Honey* were just a few stellar examples of productions with the Merrick cachet attached to them.

Yet even at the pinnacle of his amazing success, Merrick was still, at heart, the same deeply insecure, emotionally wounded youth from St. Louis. For instance, Shelagh Delaney's play *A Taste of Honey*, which opened in the East End of London in 1958 and the West End a year later, hit Merrick on a visceral, gut level—so much so that he was obsessed with bringing it to Broadway for the 1959–60 season. The play, about a young, working-class English girl who gets pregnant following a love affair with a black sailor, caused a wave of controversy when it was first staged. In this story of an abandoned, unwanted child, Merrick saw himself. Even after its initial scathing reviews in a pre-Broadway tryout in Cincinnati, Ohio, Merrick stuck to his guns—but it had nothing to do with commerce. It was all about emotion—Merrick's.

In an anecdote recounted in Howard Kissel's biography, Michael Shurtleff, who had been Merrick's casting director for many years (and the one who introduced him to future sensation Barbra Streisand for the 1962 original musical *I Can Get It for You Wholesale*), asked Merrick why he persisted in bringing *A Taste of Honey* to Broadway. "I'll tell you if you tell no one," he said. "It's the story of my life."[2]

On October 4, 1960, the play, which starred Joan Plowright (who would later marry Laurence Olivier), Angela Lansbury, and the then unknown Billy Dee Williams (as the sailor) finally made it to Broadway, where it opened at the Lyceum. The reviews were favorable and the show ran for 391 performances. During this same season, Merrick had eight shows running on the Great White Way. Sure, some of them, like *Vintage '60*, a revue that starred Bert Convy, or *The Good Soup*, with Ruth Gordon, Diane Cilento, and Mildred Natwick, had very short runs—the former ran for eight performances while the latter ran for only twenty-one performances. But these shows, like the others—including the heavyweight *Gypsy*, a holdover from two seasons before; *La Plume de Ma Tante*; *Irma La Douce* with Elliott

Gould and TV's future Herman Munster, Fred Gwynne; and *Do Re Mi*, starring Phil Silvers—were all part of the Merrick steamrolling franchise, which showed no signs of slowing down.

He Outdoes Himself

Throughout the 1960s, Merrick continued his reign as Broadway's most supreme and ubiquitous producer. He also continued to flex his muscles as Broadway's deftest and most unapologetically clever self-promoter. For *Subways Are Sleeping*, an original musical with book and lyrics by Betty Comden and Adolph Greene and music by Jule Styne, which starred Carol Lawrence, Phyllis Newman, and Orson Bean, Merrick finally outdid himself when it came to publicity stunts. The show, which opened on December 27, 1961 at the St. James, generated less than inviting reviews. The production dealt with a subject matter that was hardly conducive to lighthearted musical numbers: homelessness. To heighten public attention, Merrick devised gambits that consisted of publicly helping one vagrant (who didn't want any assistance, thank you very much) and sponsoring contests where people would win monetary prizes for taking the best photos of people sleeping on subways.

But all of these paled next to Merrick's next stunt. It was pure, anarchic genius leavened with heavy doses of irreverence and audacity. He asked one of his production assistants to bring the Manhattan telephone directory to him.

"In the phone book (and with one excursion to New Jersey), Merrick had found seven men with the same names as the [theater critics] of the seven daily papers. He had been aching to orchestrate this stunt for years, but he had had to wait until [elderly theater pundit/reviewer] Brooks Atkinson retired. There were sometimes several namesakes for the other critics, but there was only one Brooks Atkinson."[3]

Merrick ordered his press rep, Harvey Sabinson, to invite all of the individuals who had the same names as the noted theater critics to dinner either at Sardi's or the Oak Room at the Plaza Hotel, and then to the show *Subways Are Sleeping*. In exchange for this night of free luxury dining and entertainment, each person supplied a favorable comment on the show. The quotes were then printed in a full-page ad and, lest they be mistaken for the real theater critics, each person's quote was accompanied by a photo so none of the venerable theater critics could sue.

The theater community was up in arms over this stunt, considered Merrick's most outrageous. The League of American Theatres and Producers considered kicking Merrick out of their organization but relented.

Advertising VIPs at the *New York Times* and the *Tribune* were incensed. *Subways Are Sleeping* ran for 205 performances, but the myth of Merrick was escalating into the stratosphere.

Hello, Blockbuster!

Merrick's next mammoth feat in his incredible career would be realized with the January 16, 1964, opening of the classic musical *Hello, Dolly!* With a book by Michael Stewart (based on Thornton Wilder's *The Matchmaker*, which Merrick had produced in a 1955 show starring Ruth Gordon and directed by Tyrone Guthrie) and music and lyrics by Jerry Herman, the show, starring Carol Channing, became a phenomenon. Opening at the St. James, it ran for a staggering 2,844 performances, becoming one of the longest-running shows in Broadway history. After Channing left, a string of stars from Hollywood's golden age (Ginger Rogers, Betty Grable, Martha Raye) stepped into the lead role. When Pearl Bailey, the popular black entertainer, was cast as Dolly, replete with an all-black ensemble, the production got a second wind.

Years later, Merrick would attempt a similar exploit with the all-black version of *Oh, Kay!*, a tuner with music by George Gershwin and lyrics by Ira Gershwin; he had imported the show from a production he had seen at the Goodspeed Opera House in East Haddam, Connecticut. Sadly, the show, which opened on November 2, 1990, at the Richard Rodgers, would only run for 77 performances. By then Merrick's Midas touch, along with his health, was in a freefall.

During Merrick's long, esteemed career, one thing was perversely constant: the frequent scrapes he'd get into with his stars. Jackie "The Great One" Gleason of television's "Honeymooners" fame, who during the 1959–60 season starred in the Merrick-produced musical *Take Me Along* (which featured a book by Joseph Stein and Robert Russell and music and lyrics by Bob Merrill), frequently expressed his loathing of the erstwhile *Time* magazine cover subject in private—though he was quick to don a showbiz face to the press, glibly voicing his everlasting affection for Merrick. Of Merrick, Gleason said, "I made him smile once. I trained a fly to tickle his cheek."[4]

Merrick also battled with Anna Maria Alberghetti when she starred in *Carnival.* According to Howard Kissel's biography of Merrick, Alberghetti had asked to be released from her contract four months into the run after landing a film role that paid much better. Merrick refused and began a campaign against her. Not only did he rudely trash her in print, but he also enjoyed recounting an embarrassing incident with a body mic allegedly left on Alberghetti accidentally while she went to the bathroom. Soon after,

Alberghetti came down with a mysterious illness. Merrick sent her plastic roses and fired her, catapulting her understudy, Anita Gillette, into the lead.

But not everyone had a nightmarish experience working with David Merrick. The director/choreographer Gillian Lynne, for instance, relished her association with him—not just because Merrick practically launched her Broadway career, but also because she genuinely liked him. Lynne first met Merrick after he saw *Collage*, a work she choreographed (and for which Dudley Moore composed the score) at the internationally acclaimed Edinburgh Festival Theatre. It was the early 1960s and Lynne, a former ballerina, was nervously making a transition from performance to choreography. When Merrick expressed interest in bringing the Anthony Newley/Lesley Bricusse musical *The Roar of the Greasepaint—The Smell of the Crowd* to the Main Stem (Broadway), he insisted that Lynne do the choreography. "So my first producer was for the then king of Broadway, David," Lynne enthusiastically recalls.

On May 16, 1965, the show, which starred Newley (and was also directed by him), opened at the Shubert Theater, where it ran for 231 performances. For Lynne, the show was fraught with problems, none of which were connected to Merrick; all were attributable to its star and creator, Newley. Overextended and exhausted with outside engagements, Newley, who was a popular fixture in nightclubs and variety shows during the 1960s, was driving Lynne crazy over his indifference toward his performance, though he seemed to make everything else a top priority. As the opening date drew increasingly near, Lynne took Newley aside and told him he needed to shape up because his work was subpar. Newley agreed to work on his performance with Lynne the following day.

"He came in and we started working at 10 o'clock the next morning. I sent for lunch for him. We didn't stop for lunch, and at 4 o'clock, David Merrick came to me and said, 'Honestly Gillian, I think you're going to have to stop now. He's exhausted.' So I said, 'It looks like you're right.' By that time, Tony had a terrible headache and David took him to his dressing room himself, just like a father, put him to bed, and stood on guard outside his room so he would not get disturbed. That's not mean—that's not the persona of a not-very-nice man. People who didn't know him at all say that.

"He was one of the best producers I have ever known. He was very, very bright and very passionate. But he had a lawyer's mind—a very analytical mind. He was very powerful. I mean, he was terrifying for me, who had just started. It's amazing to do a little show in a festival and the next thing to find you're doing a show on Broadway. But that was the best thing about him—that he backed and fronted you."

An Unfortunate Hollywood Tryst

Merrick's rule of Broadway continued throughout the 1960s until the early seventies, when Hollywood seduced him away. Determined to carve the same indelible imprint in celluloid as he made on the stage, Merrick sought to replicate the same success with the 1972 film *Child's Play*, which boasted a screenplay by Leon Prochnik that was based on a play by Robert Marasco. Though it starred James Mason and Robert Preston and was directed by Sidney Lumet, a gifted director, the film did not fare well at the box office.

Merrick followed up with the much-overhyped *The Great Gatsby*, an adaptation of the F. Scott Fitzgerald novel. The film, which starred Mia Farrow and Robert Redford, opened in 1974 to disastrous reviews. Two mediocre films later (*Semi-Tough* and *Prime Cut*, both of which starred the then hugely popular Burt Reynolds), Merrick learned his lesson the hard way and returned to Broadway. Outside of an alleged cocaine problem, he had nothing to show for his time in Hollywood. But Merrick was hardly done yet, because what would unfold in the next chapter of his magnificent theatrical producing career was a comeback so astounding and grandiose, it would nearly eclipse his earlier accomplishments.

A True Second Act

Perhaps still imbued with the residual influence of Hollywood, Merrick became fixated on the idea of creating a theatrical musical that would rival the opulence and glamour of the old Ziegfeld productions. He zoomed in on the 1934 Warner Brothers movie musical *42nd Street* and hired most of the creative team from *Hello, Dolly!* to work on adapting it for the stage: Gower Champion, who directed Merrick's biggest smash, *Dolly*, was hired to direct, while Michael Stewart, who wrote the book for *Dolly*, was tapped to do the same for *42nd Street*; Merrick also brought in Mark Bramble as a collaborator. Except for a few additions, the Harry Warren/Al Dubin score would be the same as used in the movie.

The road to Broadway was a roller coaster ride. During its pre-Broadway tryout phase, the show played at the Kennedy Center in Washington, D.C. There it became obvious to Merrick that the show was too long and that the production elements were unappealing. Thinking the show was a major dud and that the erstwhile "indomitable showman" was now a shell of what he used to be, Merrick's investors refused to put more money into the show. But Merrick outwitted them by doing something so incredible it made jaws drop: He bought them all out. He ordered new costumes and sets, and oversaw other changes. But what he couldn't control was the health of Gower

Champion, who had been stricken with a rare form of blood cancer, to which he succumbed the morning of the Broadway opening at the Winter Garden Theatre on August 25, 1980.

Unbeknownst to the cast, Champion, whom many thought had been battling a bad flu, had been gravely ill for some time. Merrick knew of his condition but elected not to reveal it to the others. Following a standing ovation given to the cast after the opening-night performance, Merrick strode out looking grim and made a stunning announcement that would make the headlines of all the local papers: Champion had died. Supposedly Jerry Orbach, who played Julian Marsh, one of the show's leads, ordered the crew to bring the curtain down so the cast's shock and grief would not be a source of voyeuristic attention to the audience. They did, but not before Merrick, ever the master of self-promotion, had committed the ultimate coup: He parlayed a tragic death into an attention-getting event that propelled *42nd Street* into theater lore. As shameless as this ploy was, Merrick's efforts were hardly for naught: *42nd Street* ran for 3,486 performances, becoming one of the longest-running musicals in Broadway history.

Painful Memories

Unlike Gillian Lynne, Wanda Richert's memories of Merrick are infinitely more complicated and difficult to distill into simple, terse sentences. A twenty-two-year-old ingénue when she was cast as the lead, Peggy Sawyer, in the 1980 Broadway production of *42nd Street*, Richert hails Merrick as a one-of-a-kind producer: inimitable, formidable, and brilliant. But according to her, he was also a scheming, vindictive manipulator who harbored zero empathy for anyone he encountered in his path. Now a middle-aged mother and sometime performer living in Florida, Richert sees Merrick through the lens of personal emotion heavily tempered with the sobering hindsight of maturity: Shortly after landing her big break in a turn of events where life imitated art, Richert embarked on a romance with her much older director/choreographer Champion, and in her words, "watched Gower die" as *42nd Street* tap-danced its way into the annals of Broadway history. When asked to describe her first meeting with Merrick, Richert chooses her words precisely.

"It was after my first audition in New York. I had a callback that basically cemented my job in April of 1980 at the New Amsterdam. It was a couple of days before my twenty-second birthday and Gower basically handed me the role and then took me to meet David in the back of the house. So I met him in the dark, and then my dealings happened once I started rehearsals."

Richert's initial reaction to Merrick was one of fear. "He wasn't someone you engage with immediately," she recalls. "He was David Merrick."

But yet, he was a genius, and that laid the blueprint for his gargantuan success. "No matter what, he had a vision," she maintains, "and it was always, always right, bottom line. Forget everything else he did." This included taking Gower Champion's name off the advertising for *42nd Street* soon after his death. Richert was enraged and mortified.

"I was in the [production] office the day after [he did that]," she recounts. "I was on the phone with Gower's son Gregg and I was appalled at the fact that David had the audacity to do that because it was Gower Champion's *42nd Street*. The lack of respect was just mind-blowing for us. But David had no scruples. That was just pure ego." A negative instance, for sure, but it was that overinflated self-aggrandizement, fused with a mischievous joy at baiting the press, that made Merrick "the best PR person you would ever want in your life," adds Richert.

During her two-year run with *42nd Street*, *Cats* opened in October 1982 and became the hottest ticket in town. Noting this but not forgetting which show was his on the Great White Way, Merrick made one of his shrewdest moves: He bumped the opening time of the performance to 8:15 P.M. to accommodate theatergoers who may not have been able to score tickets for *Cats*. Despite her sentiments toward Merrick the man, this outrageously cheeky maneuver makes Richert chuckle to this day.

The Downfall

Soon Merrick's life would take a downward spiral from which he would never fully recover. In 1983, he suffered a debilitating stroke that left him unable to speak and in a wheelchair. He also became the center of a legal battle between his then current wife and an ex-wife over who would take care of him. Though he would produce a few more shows, including the ill-fated *Oh, Kay!*, none would ever reach the dizzying heights of *Gypsy, Hello, Dolly!*, or *42nd Street*. His time as the king of Broadway was over and all that was left was the troubled legend.

But not all was moribund for Merrick in the last chapter of his life. Two years before he died in 2000, he created the David Merrick Arts Foundation to support the ongoing development of an indigenous art form that had been so near and dear to him—the American musical. However, Howard Kissel, in his Merrick biography, places the date of the inception of the foundation much earlier—1959. According to Kissel, the foundation largely financed *Gypsy* and created a backlog of funds that could be drawn upon to invest in less commercial productions. Whenever the foundation began, it was still a wise move for Merrick, buffering him against flops and Uncle Sam, especially because the capital drawn from it could not be taxed.

Like Ziegfeld, his childhood hero, and Joe Papp, his professional rival, Merrick was a colorful, multilayered, towering auteur who left an ineradicable stamp on everything and everyone he touched. As one of Broadway's most ruthless, vociferous, and cantankerous proponents, there's no doubt Merrick was difficult, but he was a great producer.

In 2001, a year after his death, Merrick was inducted into the St. Louis Walk of Fame, an ironic epitaph considering how hard he tried to distance himself from his roots when he first landed in New York sixty years earlier. In the end, he would be embraced more readily by St. Louis than by the Broadway community, where he still, at press time, has not been inducted into the American Theatre Hall of Fame.

Career Highlights

- Trained as a lawyer but never practiced
- Brought publicity stunts and self-promotion to a new level
- Introduced British playwrights such as John Osborne and Tom Stoppard to the American theater
- Founded the David Merrick Arts Foundation to support the development of American musicals
- Became the most famous Broadway producer in the 1950s and 1960s
- Made the cover of the March 25, 1966 issue of *Time* magazine
- Cast Barbra Streisand in her first Broadway role in *I Can Get It for You Wholesale*
- Notable productions include *Fanny*, *Gypsy*, *Look Back in Anger*, *Becket*, *Irma La Douce*, *Oliver!*, *Hello, Dolly!*, and *42nd Street*

End Notes

1. From Howard Kissel's *David Merrick: The Abominable Showman: An Unauthorized Biography*, Applause Books, 1993.
2. From *David Merrick: The Abominable Showman.*
3. From *David Merrick: The Abominable Showman.*
4. From *David Merrick: The Abominable Showman.*

SECTION II
Old World

CHAPTER 4
Roger Berlind

"The most respected producer on Broadway."

—Roger Horchow, producer

Roger Berlind (left) and John Bolton

The Gentleman Connoisseur

He was one of the founders of an investment banking company that would later morph into Citigroup, formerly considered one of the world's largest firms in terms of net profits and assets. He is on Lehman Brothers' board of directors, has served as a trustee at Princeton University, his alma mater, and spent much of his life working on Wall Street, where the former English major built a highly lucrative career for himself. But all of this would come to a dramatic halt when Berlind entered his forties.

Following a personal tragedy in his life, the details of which he is loath to reveal, Berlind left the world of high finance and entered one that he had dallied with twice in his youth. When he was a college student he acted in and directed productions with Princeton's renowned Triangle Club. Later on, after serving a stint in the Army, he did a brief—and unsuccessful—spell as a songwriter before investment banking beckoned. The theater bug now bit him again, this time courtesy of a fortuitous meeting with musical theater legend Richard Rodgers, whose catalog of songs had already been seared in Berlind's memory.

Goodbye Wall Street, Hello Broadway

"[Rodgers and I] hit it off and he had a new show, *Rex*, with Nicol Williamson. I signed on as an assistant associate producer and traveled with the show. That was successful, but I thought, 'Hmm, I could produce as well as these guys,' so I started producing."

Joan Marcus

Stephen Campbell Moore and Dominic Cooper in the 2006 Tony Award–winning production of *The History Boys*. The show scored yet another success, both critical and commercial, for Roger Berlind, one of its Broadway producers.

It was 1976, the year of the United States bicentennial. Berlind went to work on his first producing project, *Music Is*, a tuner that featured a book by George Abbott, lyrics by Will Holt, and a score by Richard Adler. The production, which originally premiered at Seattle Repertory Theatre, cost about $800,000, an exorbitant sum for a musical in those days. According to Berlind, the funds were supplied not only by the Seattle Rep, but by investors who were also personal friends. Unfortunately, nothing was recouped. The show, which opened on Broadway on December 20, 1976, at the St. James Theater, ran only for eight performances; it was a flop. Back to the drawing board.

Success At Last

It wouldn't be too long before Berlind experienced his first major success as a Broadway producer. Four years after the *Music Is* debacle, Berlind took on a play he deemed to have little commercial prospects—in fact, he was doing it expressly for art's sake. The show was Peter Shaffer's *Amadeus*.

Directed by Peter Hall and starring Ian McKellen, Tim Curry, and Jane Seymour in the original Broadway cast, the play was loosely based on the lives of composers Wolfgang Amadeus Mozart and Antonio Salieri and their supposed rivalry. Berlind and Gerald Schoenfeld, chairman of the Shubert Organization, which was Broadway's largest theater owner (and producer of a multitude of productions), had seen the show in London. They ended up partnering up with McCann/Nugent, a producing organization founded by Elizabeth McCann and Nellie Nugent, to produce the British import on the Great White Way. Opening on December 17, 1980, at the Broadhurst Theater, *Amadeus* would run for 1,181 performances and win a slew of Tony Awards, among them Best Play, Best Actor (Ian McKellen), and Best Direction of a Play (Peter Hall).

If *Amadeus* had been a watershed in Berlind's career as a producer, then his next show, *Sophisticated Ladies*, an original revue showcasing the music of Duke Ellington, would solidify his emerging reputation as a producer of quality shows that were achieving the paradox: They were making money. But the journey to Broadway would be a taxing ordeal.

"*Sophisticated Ladies* was a very tough show to do. What we opened with in Philadelphia [in an early pre-Broadway tryout] was totally inadequate: We had to get new costumes. We also had to bring in another choreographer and another director. We stopped after Washington, D.C., and went back into rehearsal before coming to New York. [Prior to Broadway] the show was fraught with tensions and conflicts, and then we got it right. Two days before we opened [on March 1, 1981, at the Lunt-Fontanne Theatre], I suddenly felt that this was going to work. But there was a very tough road to get there."

The show, which ran for 767 performances, was a hit. Like Berlind's previous project, *Amadeus, Sophisticated Ladies* walked off with two Tonys, one for Best Featured Actor in a Musical (Hinton Battle) and the other for Best Costume Design (Willa Kim). The quiet, well-mannered, erstwhile Wall Street wizard was on a roll. His next project, *Nine*, a musical adaptation of the Fellini movie *8½*, would also score well commercially and artistically, bringing home Tonys for Best Musical, Best Original Score (Maury Yeston), Best Featured Actress in a Musical (Liliane Montevecchi), and Best Direction of a Musical (Tommy Tune).

Berlind's early years as a producer may have been dogged by uncertainty, but now, after being attached to a string of successes, he was batting a strong average of hits versus misses. Yet the challenges of producing remain the same for him now as then.

Making Sense of It All

"It's trying to make sense out of a basically senseless business and creating an economic model for a particular show: a capital budget or operating budget, hiring all the people you need to put on a show, the public relations firm, the advertising agency, the general manager, getting the right insurance, negotiating with a variety of people—unions. [laughs] It's a complicated business for one that has relatively small economic results."

Dealing with agents of creative personnel (actors, directors, designers, composers, etc.) is, according to Berlind, the worst albeit necessary part of his job. And it's not just because they want more money for their clients than the production budget can possibly afford.

"It's all the other accoutrements that go into a contract—the flights, first class versus business class. They all have economic implications but they can get pretty detailed. And of course, the original rights acquisitions are subject to the Dramatists Guild's approval, which is an arbitrary kind of backstop for the writer's agents to hide behind while the Dramatists Guild has to approve the contract. The same thing is true with the director and choreographer of a musical and the Society of Stage Directors and Choreographers that represents them. Then there are the designers and their own guilds. And the unions—Actors' Equity and the stagehands and the musicians. You have to conform to their view of what the weather is like. It's a complex business and you have a lot of people to deal with. You have a lot of contracts and negotiating. The only real interest for me is helping create what goes onstage. To get to that point, there are lots of problems to deal with."

To resolve issues that may be stalling the progress of a show, Berlind does have to exert control and make difficult decisions, such as firing certain staffers, but he is never a tyrant. In fact, he reveals that one reason why producers like to have him on their team is because "I'm a benign presence and I'm easy to get along with." This amiable flexibility on Berlind's part makes him also very amenable to the creative talent that works on his productions.

As a producer, one very difficult decision he may face is when to close a show that is consistently losing money. Berlind concedes that it's never easy to do this "but when the handwriting is on the wall, it's only ego that keeps you running while you're slowly using up capital that doesn't necessarily belong to you. You have to know when to close."

However, there are instances where it might be advantageous for a show that's not raking in the big bucks at the box office to stay open—providing "you're not getting killed each week." The reasons would be to heighten the road possibilities as well as build up the stock and amateur rights.

A Class Act

William Ivey Long, the multiple Tony Award–winning costume designer from the South whose dazzling and often flamboyant confections have been the visual highlights of many shows, ranks Berlind high on his list of producers. "He's very understanding of the creative souls in the process," says Long, who first worked with Berlind on the original production of *Nine* back in 1982. It was one of the first Broadway shows that the Yale Drama School grad worked on. Professionally, *Nine* was a high point for Long because not only did he win the first of many Tonys for his costume designs, but it was the inception of a long and rewarding association with Berlind, whom he admires enormously.

"Well, everyone says he's such a gentleman ... and although his approach has never been from the trenches," adds Long, "he has that wonderful connoisseurship [that enables him to produce] from that slightly observing perspective. This allows you to talk to him in a different way. [I've always found him] very appreciative. It's wonderful working with him."

Berlind's easygoing nature may be the antithesis to the old, traditional archetype of the producer as a control-hungry despot, perhaps best represented in our list of producers by David Merrick. Berlind feels that's a model that no longer exists in the current Broadway marketplace—it ended with Merrick (whom Berlind did know). "You can't be [a tyrant] anymore," he insists.

Is it because of economics and the increasing sophistication of modern audiences?

"I think it's a combination of factors," answers Berlind. "[Merrick's] results weren't that great. I guess Alexander Cohen was kind of that tradition but I liked Alexander Cohen. Good fellow. But [working under] a certain

Julianne Moore and Bill Nighy in *The Vertical Hour*. Although the show received mixed reviews and closed before the end of its limited engagement, supposedly it recouped its investment.

presumption of superiority and feeling that I'm in control and what I say counts—I think the writer and director are in charge, facilitating what they do."

Berlind's attraction to first-rate material greatly informs his decisions as to which projects to pursue and produce. "Maybe my tastes are too elevated for general consumption," he admits, "but I like to go with plays that have more meat, if you will, that are about something serious and have artistic and intellectual hopes. Maybe it's already in the script. Not that I'm averse to a flat-out comedy that's very, very funny. There's no real rule of thumb. I go by gut instinct. But there are things I don't like, which are jukebox musicals and song compilations."

Sometimes It's Art That Counts

His propensity for championing exceptional work has had its share of financial drawbacks. Berlind, who was one of the producers of *Caroline, or Change*, the 2004 musical featuring a book by Tony Kushner and a score by Jeanine Tesori (see the Margo Lion chapter on page 85), says the show "was an example of a musical that had to fight its way to get on and didn't do well here." (He goes on to point out that it recently won the Evening Standard Theatre Award in London for Best Musical.) Berlind did get involved with the project even though he did harbor strong doubts that it would recoup, which it did not. So why did he get behind the ill-fated *Caroline, or Change*?

"You do it because that's part of being in the business and you want to support certain writers and you want to support a script that deserves production even though its prospects are very limited from an economic standpoint.... Usually, with the serious plays I do, I don't expect to do well economically." This from a man whose last four serious plays—Michael Frayn's *Copenhagen*, David Auburn's *Proof*, John Patrick Shanley's *Doubt*, and Alan Bennett's *The History Boys*—not only won Tonys for Best Play but were all big hits. (*Proof* and *Doubt* also had national tours, which shocks Berlind because he never expects that result from a serious play.)

Even with shows where Berlind thinks there might be a possibility of recouping, he does give disclaimers "in big bold letters" to investors beforehand. "Every document they get harps upon the fact that most shows don't make it." However, for a show that he thinks will not work, Berlind invests in it himself and does not solicit backers. "I only raise money for shows that I think are going to be commercially successful."

So if the odds are inexorably stacked against most shows hitting Broadway, why does Berlind persist as a legit producer?

"I think I can beat the averages," he says with the forthright confidence of someone who spent half of his life carving a profitable niche for himself in the high-risk world of Wall Street. "In fact, I just went through the last forty-six shows I did [and estimated that] exactly twenty-three shows were successful economically and twenty-three were not. That's a 50 percent batting average—not bad."

But you don't become a producer just because you want to make money, says Berlind. If that's the case, then you're better off going to Wall Street. "All of the producers I know are interested in the art of it. Maybe they're frustrated writers or directors or they got a taste of the bug in college. They are doing it out of that love."

When asked if he feels that his high-finance background informs his work as a producer, Berlind says it absolutely does. "The risk-reward is something you're briefed on. It's more akin to venture capital than to other traditional forms of investment banking. What I read is that only one out of five, whether it's wildcatting for oil or starting a new company or putting on a show, is supposed to be successful."

Working in a Team
When undertaking a new project, Berlind either options the rights or aligns himself with someone who already has the rights. He did the latter with his most recent show, David Hare's *The Vertical Hour*, which starred film actress Julianne Moore (in her Broadway debut) and British actor Bill Nighy and

opened for a limited run at the Music Box Theatre during the 2006–07 season. Scott Rudin, who has worked with Berlind on a vast number of shows, was the lead producer who developed the project.

Working with another producer or a team does reap some positive dividends. "You share a risk and you share a reward. If you know you have a good working relationship with other producers, it's very easy to join in if you like the product."

Other projects that have recently come up the pipeline for Berlind include the stage adaptation of Joan Didion's highly acclaimed book, *The Year of Magical Thinking*, a memoir that deals with the aftermath of the death of Didion's husband, writer John Gregory Dunne, and starred Vanessa Redgrave; and the Tony Award–nominated Kander/Ebb musical *Curtains*, starring David Hyde Pierce of TV's *Frasier* fame.

Berlind got involved with *The Year of Magical Thinking* courtesy of Rudin, who was also the lead producer on this project. Rudin, who was friends with Dunne, asked Didion if she would be interested in turning her book into a play and worked with her in developing it. Berlind joined the producing team because he liked the book very much.

When I interviewed Berlind in late 2006, he was very excited about the impending Broadway arrival of *Curtains*, in which he played a more proactive role in developing for the boards ("It's very funny and I'm very enthusiastic about it"). *Curtains* opened (and that is no pun) on Broadway on March 22, 2007, at the Al Hirschfeld Theatre. Hyde Pierce took home a Tony Award a few months later for Best Actor in a Musical.

Roger Horchow, who coproduced *Kiss Me Kate* with Berlind and is also coproducing *Curtains*, believes Berlind's proficient negotiation skills, combined with his utter diplomacy and mild sense of humor, helped seal the deal to bring the show to the Old Rialto in 2007. The project, which had been originally produced by the Center Theatre Group and staged in Los Angeles' Ahmanson Theatre for a brief run, was not an easy one to move due to a number of factors.

"It was very complicated because the Center Theatre Group had certain rights," explains Horchow. "I would say his producing skills are the best there is because he achieved an association with them that was satisfactory to them and to us—and profitable for both of us. Roger conceived of the idea of how to work with them and enhanced their production (i.e., their costumes and their sets) so they would be Broadway movable, which required, 'We'll pay this and you pay this and you get back this if this achieves this and we'll split if this happens,' and so forth, so he did all of that. But it all happened because of Roger's skill—his foresight in seeing how it might work."

One Regret

Was there ever a project that Berlind passed on that he now regrets dismissing? Yes, but it wasn't so much that he passed on it—there was never an opportune moment for him to produce it. It dealt with several relationships set against the early years of the AIDS crisis. The play? *Angels in America*, the masterwork by Tony Kushner.

"I was once part of a team at the Kennedy Center [in D.C.]. Roger Stevens [the late theatrical producer who served as chairman of the National Endowment for the Arts] started to encourage new play development by giving grants to different theaters around the country that would submit plays. There were about 200 or 300 plays that would come in. They would screen out 40. [*Angels in America* survived the cut.] Everybody adored it but then when it went on a commercial track, I was too busy doing something else and there were already twenty people on it—a very large number of people wanted to coproduce it. I don't like being one of a mass producing group because it's noisy. I was tied up with other things but I'm glad it was successful."

Berlind's advice to aspiring producers is grounded in the same no-nonsense business mindset that formerly got a strenuous workout in the pressure-cooker of investment banking early in his life. "Go to Wall Street. [laughs] You have to be committed, slightly insane, and willing to go through that and recognize that this is not a bed of roses. You have to approach it professionally because there are things you can learn. CTI (*www.commercialtheaterinstitute.com*) runs a [three-day or fourteen-week] course on producing that you should take. You should read the Dramatists Guild contract as well as the Actors' Equity manual and learn all the basics of things you're going to do. And then recognize that you're going to have to pony up some capital—either have it yourself or have people rely on your judgment and invest with you. It's generally better to start with smaller, nonprofit theaters—they are wonderful training grounds. New York is full of them; so is the whole country. Starting and learning about what goes into putting on a show is the way to do it instead of running from Wall Street or whatever your business is and jumping into producing for Broadway. I think it's better to learn the ropes."

Career Highlights

- Trained as an investment banker
- Sits on the board of directors for Lehman Brothers
- The Roger S. Berlind Theatre at the McCarter Theatre Center in Princeton, New Jersey, opened in 2003, is named after him.

- Became a producer midlife (First Broadway show he worked on as a producer was the 1976 musical *Rex*, which featured music by Richard Rodgers and lyrics by Sheldon Harnick; the show opened on April 25 and closed a month and a half later on June 5)
- His Broadway productions have garnered over 60 Tony Awards, 12 for Best Production (Won his first Tony in 1981 for *Amadeus*)
- Produced *Curtains* in 2007, the last Kander/Ebb musical to be staged on Broadway following Fred Ebb's death

courtesy of Encores

CHAPTER 5
Jack Viertel

"Jack is a positive force, a huge fan of the art form and the people who put it together. . . . He knows the challenges but yet at the same time, he has respect for the craft."

—John Rando, director (*Urinetown*, *The Wedding Singer*)

Jack Viertel

The Dramaturg

When Jack Viertel, the creative director of Jujamcyn Theaters, was a child, he knew he wanted to be in the theater. The catch is he wanted to be in the audience, not necessarily on the stage. The revelation came to him while watching a 1955 Broadway production of *Peter Pan* starring legendary leading lady Mary Martin. He was almost six years old and found himself utterly transfixed by the magic unfolding before him. Except for occasional thoughts of the Yankees, theater became Viertel's all-consuming obsession.

Early Addiction

Viertel's fixation shouldn't have been surprising given that theater was already in his lineage. His father, Joseph, wrote a play, *So Proudly We Hail*, which opened on Broadway in 1936. And in the early part of the 20th century, Viertel's grandfather, Jack Shapiro, had worked as a contractor, building several Broadway theaters. He ended up owning one briefly during the Depression after the original owner couldn't pay for it. There in the theater, initially named the Earl Carroll and later known as the French Casino, Viertel's grandfather would produce lavish *Folies Bergère*–type shows.

As a teen, Viertel, aided and abetted by his parents' encouragement, fed his addiction by making regular trips to New York City from his home in Connecticut to see both Broadway and off-Broadway shows. Starting in 1962, when he was thirteen, up through 1967, Viertel's passion for theatergoing was insatiable. He couldn't get enough of it and he saw everything there was to see.

Even his choice of prep school—Pomfret School in Connecticut—was reflective of this budding passion. "They produced five plays a year, as opposed to some of the more conservative schools that only produced one," he recalls. Later, as a student at Harvard, Viertel briefly flirted with acting, but soon realized it was a vocation not well suited for him. Witnessing the turbulence of the late 1960s, Viertel began to feel that theater, especially Broadway, was irrelevant. He soon withdrew from theater and started to devote his energies to a local radio station, where he headed the folk music department.

Yet even during those heady times, theater still exerted a vestigial hold on the once besotted young man. At the radio station, he hosted a theater music show every week, focusing on original cast albums.

So what pulled the future dramatic critic turned dramaturg turned producer back into theater's seductive fold? Two words: Stephen Sondheim. "*Company* and *Follies* brought me back. [Both shows were playing] right around the same time. I hadn't gone to the theater for a few years until [old Harvard classmate and future *New York Times* theater critic] Frank Rich dragged me to see *Company* [which was having a tryout in Boston].

"I've always been a big Sondheim fan. He had sort of disappeared after *Anyone Can Whistle*. He didn't write another show until *Company*, although he did the lyrics for *Do I Hear a Waltz?* [which had music by Richard Rodgers and a book by Arthur Laurents]. Then he came back with a vengeance. *Company* and *Follies*, which followed each other by almost exactly a year, were so much of that time in terms of how edgy they were and how much they reflected the national angst and bleak mood that we were all living in. Suddenly, through Sondheim, Broadway did seem relevant again."

After relocating to Los Angeles, Viertel worked as a freelance writer and soon landed his first job in the theater—as a drama critic. "I told you I wanted to be in the audience," Viertel jokes. He had gotten a call from one of his college chums telling him that a friend had started an L.A. edition of the *Chicago Reader* and the paper was looking for a theater critic. What followed next set into motion events that would be pivotal to Viertel's career as a theater producer.

"I called the guy and told him I know something about the theater," he recounts. "He told me, 'We're paying $35 for every review we publish.' That sounded like a good deal for me. Then I called the publicist for *Annie*, which was making a national tour stop at L.A. at the Shubert Theater. That was my first published theater review! I wrote for the *Reader* at $35 a week for a couple of years.

"Then I got a call from the *Herald Examiner*, which was like the L.A. equivalent to the *New York Daily News*. It was kind of a blue-collar paper," continues Viertel. The *Examiner* wanted to speak to him about replacing its theater critic, who was retiring. "It had never occurred to me that I would earn a living being a theater critic, but I went down there. They said, 'Can you bring your portfolio?' I thought, What portfolio? Then I realized that over the course of three years, I had built up a lot of theater writing. So I went to the morgue at the *Reader*. With scissors, I started clipping and Xeroxing and brought them a portfolio. They hired me. Suddenly at the age of thirty, I was earning a living working at a newspaper."

From the late seventies through the mid-1980s, Viertel worked as a drama critic for the *Herald Examiner*. The position was fine; management and fellow staffers treated Viertel well. But there was one problem: Viertel didn't want to spend the rest of his life at a newspaper, and he realized this after he was promoted to arts editor.

Carol Rosegg

Harry Lennix in *Radio Golf*, the last play written by August Wilson

Making a Transition

"Although it was a great honor and a privilege, I wasn't actually interested in the newspaper business. I had only become a theater critic because I was interested in the theater. So I thought, Gee, if I do this job, then they'll make me a city editor or a managing editor and I'll be in the newspaper business. I don't want to be in the newspaper business."

To prevent that from happening, Viertel spoke to Gordon Davidson, then artistic director of the Mark Taper Forum, about replacing the dramaturg who was leaving his post. "I was looking to start my life in a different way," he says. "So it all worked out."

What exactly is a dramaturg? "It's only definable in terms of what kind of dramaturg you are," he explains. "A dramaturg at the Mark Taper Forum, which is the only one I've ever been, was a kind of an associate artistic director. I did a lot of program writing, a lot of playbill writing, and a lot of reading of scripts that had made their way through the literary management machine up to the point where they needed serious discussion. I worked with a lot of playwrights on new plays. We had a new-play festival that happened every other year and we had new plays in our mainstage season. Gordon Davidson was a relentless believer in continuing to work on plays even if they already had been on Broadway or off-Broadway. I really tried to work with artists from working at the paper. So it was all of those things."

Fate intervened yet again two years later with a job offer that both astounded and confounded Viertel. He had gotten a call from Rocco Landesman, who had just been named president of Jujamcyn Theaters.

"My only connection to him had been that I had written a terrible review of *Big River*, which had been trying out at the La Jolla Playhouse. Rocco had actually credited me with saying some things about the show that had helped him fix it. Then he and his then wife Heidi invited me to see *Into the Woods* when it was at the Old Globe, which was his next production, even though I was no longer a critic, just to see if I liked it and if I had anything smart to say about that show. So I called Rocco and he said, "I have taken over this theater chain. Do you want to come work here?" I said, "Why would you want me to come work there?" He said, "Well, you wrote this terrible review that had some valuable information." So I came and worked for Jujamcyn.

"[Rocco asked me if I] want to be called a vice president. I said no, I like to be called a creative director, which is a title I invented. I didn't realize this is a very common title in the advertising world and various other places. I thought I had this brilliant inspiration. Basically, Rocco hired me because in 1987 when he took over Jujamcyn, it had become the court of last resort for producers who wanted to put on a new play on Broadway. We owned five theaters, which made us the smallest, and they weren't the most prestigious theaters; in some cases, they were difficult theaters to work in. The *street* was dead, so our theaters were empty, because everybody's theaters were sort of empty—but we were the emptiest of them all."

John Earl Jelks and Anthony Chisolm in *Radio Golf*

Jim Binger, who owned Jujamcyn, hired Rocco to try to figure out a way to make them successful. "What Rocco pitched to him was that the only way to make it successful would be to produce our own work, because what was at that time the most successful trend on Broadway was English megamusicals," says Viertel. "The Shubert Organization and the Nederlander Organization had much better relationships with Cameron Mackintosh, Andrew Lloyd Webber, and the people who were doing those shows in London. We didn't have any relationships in London really. Rocco said we were never going to win those competitions; the only way to fill these theaters was to be our own tenant. Jim accepted that idea and Rocco said he needed someone to be on the firing line to do all that." Hence, his hiring of Jack Viertel.

Lights of Broadway

As creative director of Jujamcyn, Viertel's responsibilities are threefold. First, keep an eye on what is going on at the nonprofit theaters across the country and maybe invest in shows—or, to use a term commonly employed in the industry, "enhance" them with the possible aim of moving them to the Great White Way. Second, come up with ideas for original musicals, commission them to a resident theater or workshop. Third, act as a handicapper when producers of other shows come to Viertel for the express purpose of wanting to move them into a Jujamcyn theater. The latter responsibility makes Viertel seem like a booking agent for Jujamcyn, but with the economics of producing a Broadway show becoming so costly, it's one that he's grown to be more familiar with as of late, as opposed to producing a show from the outset.

"I've done all three jobs for almost the last twenty years, but as the street has gotten more and more successful, our theaters have gotten more and more frequently lit and booked more because there is no risk in booking," he admits. "When you produce, you actually sink a million or two million dollars in something. At the moment, I could do more handicapping and less producing, which I like less, but it makes sense from a business point of view."

Viertel does get involved with raising capital for a production but, he adds pointedly, "You can't put up all the money yourself. You need partners, so you go out and find partners. I've done very little in the way of actually going out to individual investors and saying, give us $10,000 or $20,000. I've done a lot of going out to partners and saying, commit to $750,000. Then you go out and figure out how to raise it."

Viertel and Jujamcyn are very honest to potential backers when it comes to the likely possibility that they may not recoup. But, he emphasizes, the donors are usually people who have invested capital in productions before and are cognizant of the risks involved. Plus, if they can afford to put up a half million or a million dollars for a show, then they probably can risk losing it all.

"People who want to do this want to do it for all kinds of reasons. One of the reasons is never because they think it's a safe investment. They like it; they want to be part of it in some way or the other. The investment papers we send out to people are very clear about defining what the risks are."

Viertel's first producing project for Jujamcyn was *M. Butterfly*, a script he had taken with him from the Taper when he first landed his creative director job. (Though *Into the Woods* was already in rehearsals and almost in previews when he arrived at Jujamcyn, according to Viertel, he had not really worked on it, except for some discussions with its director, James Lapine, who also wrote the book, about some issues to work out.) He worked on *M. Butterfly* actively from its inception to completion. "Stuart Ostrow, who was the initiating producer, was looking for investment and for a theater," relates Viertel. "We committed to doing it right away when I got here."

M. Butterfly opened March 20, 1988, at the Eugene O'Neill Theater, and closed on January 27, 1990. It ran for 777 performances. The show reaped critical raves. At the 1988 Tony Awards, *M. Butterfly* playwright David Henry Hwang won Broadway's highest honor for Best Play (a year later, he would win the Pulitzer Prize for Drama, also for *M. Butterfly*), while director John Dexter picked up a trophy for Best Direction of a Play.

An Angelic Headache

One of Viertel's most rewarding—and problematic—projects was producing both parts of *Angels in America* (*Millennium Approaches* and *Perestroika*). The sheer logistics and epic quality of Kushner's mammoth opus were enough to induce a migraine. (For coproducer Margo Lion's perspective on producing this two-part show, please turn to the chapter on her starting on page 85.)

"Because it was a two-part play and each part was three and a half hours long, the process of actually producing it threw up challenges that even I didn't understand when we started. We committed to doing both because Tony Kushner said, 'I want both of them done and I'm really not interested in doing just one. So if you're really only interested in doing part one, let me go find some other producers.' We wanted to do the plays, so we said, 'No, we'll commit to doing both.' So because the second part wasn't really finished, we didn't really know what we were getting into. We were able to produce the first part before the [writing for the] second one was finished. The first one was up and running. When it came time to put the second one into rehearsal with the same cast, because each of them was three and a half hours long, you couldn't rehearse a full day and perform at night. We had to start canceling performances, having half-day rehearsals and then having performances. Then when it came time to actually getting the second one into the theater, we had to stop doing the first one, then tech the second one.... It was completely thrilling from the minute we started working up until the day it closed. But it was mystifyingly complicated.

"What was so wonderful and yet frightening about it is that you had a feeling that you were never ever going to work on something of this magnitude again. Yet it wasn't perfect and it wasn't finished and there were parts of it that didn't work. But there was this weird sense of, we got to get this thing better than it is, but it's the greatest play written already. It was very odd."

The other project—or succession of projects—that Viertel expresses profound pride in is his involvement in producing all six of the last plays of the late playwright August Wilson. "Just being part of that whole journey as each of them traveled around the country, getting ready to come to Broadway, and getting to know August and working with him, was an equally satisfying experience, but [unlike *Angels in America*] it was spread out over a much longer period of time."

With a Studied Eye

Viertel believes that his background as a drama critic and dramaturg informs what he does as a producer. Because he did both for so long, it is easy for him, unlike other producers, to stand back and view the proceedings with a studied, impartial eye. In many ways, this makes him feel like he's standing on the periphery of the action, witnessing everything through the prism of an outsider. Viertel's propensity for critical analysis has been a great asset when evaluating the strengths and liabilities in a show, either in gestation or already in previews.

"You get seduced by the rehearsal process. I've tried to remain outside that process as much as it seems healthy simply because it's important to retain an objective view. Because I spent all those years trying to write articulately about what worked and didn't work in plays, I feel a responsibility as a producer to retain that articulateness to the degree that I have any and to communicate with the artists. Learning how to do that without being high-handed or insulting or engendering more hostility than usefulness has been a lifelong process."

Viertel's criteria for choosing a project are strongly predicated upon how much affection he has for the material. On the other hand, his criteria for booking a project into a Jujamcyn theater might have more to do with business and less to do with personal sentiment.

"[When choosing a project to produce], there are four or five things I really focus on to try to figure out if something can work," notes Viertel. "First of all, is it a story that delivers to the audience what the audience came to get? Is it a satisfying tale told, if that's what it is? That's criterion number one. Criterion number two is—and these get more venal as they go along—does it, like *Angels in America*, for instance, interface with the world that we live in a way that people are already talking about or that they want to talk about? Does it have the opportunity to be newsy in that way? Number three: Does it have a role in it that will either give a star or someone who will give a star performance an opportunity to give a live performance that people will want to see? Finally, is it a manageable financial arrangement that can be made? In other words, it's very hard to produce a play that has thirty-five people in it or a play that has extraordinary theatrical demands unless you can figure out how to do them in a reasonable amount of time and for a reasonable amount of money."

Viertel says these questions also factor strongly into his decision to book a show into a Jujamcyn theater. However, the passion and enthusiasm for this type of "product"—a term Viertel is loath to use to describe shows he books—will be comparatively less than for a show he's produced. Frequently, when Jujamcyn theaters are full, it's often a question of weighing one show against the other. Still, because Jujamcyn is running a business in which, in addition to being theater producers, they're also theater operators and owners, it's rare that a production will not be booked into one of their venues "unless you think you might get arrested or the theater might fall down."

It does help if the show's creative team has a tried and true résumé. "This is Broadway . . . the highest level of production you want to experience in America, and you want experienced people at the helm. You have less risk of abject embarrassment or amateurishness if you hire people who've done this a lot," says Viertel. "That's not to say that there aren't really talented people coming up in the world. They are, but usually if you look at a show like *Spring Awakening*, [it] has an inventive new group of people doing it, however [director] Michael Mayer has been there before. He's not an amateur. The most exciting shows come from the mix of experience and new inspiration."

Standing Encore

Concurrent to Viertel's duties at Jujamcyn is his post as artistic director of Encores, which showcases unknown and obscure musicals of the Golden Age of Broadway, with minimal production values but maximal orchestrations. Viertel arrived at this title after spending nearly a decade on the advisory board. During that time, Encores had a succession of artistic directors, Walter Bobbie and Kathleen Marshall, both of whom would win Tony Awards for their respective efforts—he for his direction of *Chicago* and she for her choreography of recent Broadway revivals of *The Pajama Game* and *Wonderful Town*. Bobbie and Marshall left Encores once they became far too busy with their theater careers.

Ted Chapin, who runs The Rodgers and Hammerstein Organization, had asked Viertel if he'd like to assume artistic stewardship of Encores. Though he had been approached several years earlier, Viertel still felt green with his position at Jujamcyn. But now the timing was just right: "I understood my job at Jujamcyn better and what the limitations of my ability to spend time with Encores would be. I was able to work out a deal with both."

Broadway director John Rando, who first met Viertel briefly fifteen years ago but got to know him very well when he began helming productions at Encores, feels Viertel's knowledge of dramatic structure make him both a supportive producer and respectful one.

"Jack truly understands, especially in the musical theater world and in the legitimate play world, the construction of plays and musicals," says Rando, who won a Tony for his direction of *Urinetown*. "He knows intimately how they're assembled and why they work. He's able to read scripts and help create them because of this kind of in-depth knowledge. For example, when I recently worked with him on the Encores production of *Face the Music*, we knew we wanted to do this piece, but it was very flawed when it was handed to us. It hadn't been done since 1932. Also closely working with me was Rob Fisher, the musical conductor, and David Ives, who was going to revise the book. Jack encouraged us to find a stronger arc in the story and to make use of some of the songs that were cut before it ever arrived on Broadway.

"Same thing with *The Wedding Singer.* Jack can certainly talk about actors and production values and all that, but he has a very keen sense of how to pinpoint a flaw in a story and can give constructive criticism on how to build a better play. He is a gentleman and has a terrific demeanor in terms of how to deal with artists . . . and the daunting task that we have when we put on a show and try to make it work."

What Viertel enjoys most about his job at Jujamcyn is partaking of the creative process. Working with artists, seeing the process evolve from casting to previews to opening night, and noting the improvements made every step of the way are high points for Viertel. What he dislikes is attending to business issues following opening night, such as marketing/advertising and having to replace actors eventually, even if the show turns out to be a smash success. In a perfect world, Viertel would love to be involved up until the show is put on its feet, where he can see it occasionally before setting his sights on a new project; unfortunately, that doesn't happen in the real world.

When Viertel first becomes interested in a project, he does one of two things: If it's a play, he calls the playwright's agent; if it's a musical, then usually the idea comes first and it'll be up to Viertel and Jujamcyn to decide who will write it, in what style it'll be penned, and who will direct it. Producing musicals on Broadway is more "proactive" than producing plays, says Viertel, because plays are "largely imported from somewhere, not necessarily overseas."

With so many promising playwrights extant, why is this the case? Viertel's answer is blunt and consistent with the responses made on this subject by our other producers: "It's because no one is prepared to take the risk of producing a play cold on Broadway when you don't have to. If I read a script that I'm interested in, I can get on the phone with the Seattle Repertory Theatre and ask them if they want to do this together, and for the fraction of the price, you'll find out whether it's as good as you think it is. So why would you not take advantage of that?"

Take a Starlet to Lunch

When asked what qualities all good producers should possess, the urbane and shrewd Viertel is succinct—and upfront—in his reply: "taste, energy, passion, and access to money." In Viertel's case, those characteristics seem to be inborn, rather than developed—with the exception of the latter one, of course.

Viertel's advice to aspiring producers is based on what he knows and what has worked effectively for him in his nearly two-decade reign as creative director of the Jujamcyn Theaters. "I think that the one thing that many, many producers lack is any real dramaturgical skills, which can be learned. There are structural and emotional ways of telling a story that are not rocket science. They are a little bit mysterious, but they're really not; it takes time and effort to learn where things go right and where they go wrong. In my experience that's the area [I specialize in]. I don't mean to toot my own horn because there are plenty of things I'm bad at. But that's an area where I'm working with producers who don't really get it. They are very good at other things, like raising money. They understand marketing and advertising. I knew one older producer in California: His great gift to the world was that he knew how to take a starlet to lunch, which is how a lot of those people ended up in shows. While it seems like a fatuous gift, it's an essential gift. Somebody has got to get Rosalind Russell to do the shows. I can't do that very well. But I do understand when a story is going wrong and how it's going wrong."

Career Highlights

- Attended Harvard with classmate and future *New York Times* theater critic Frank Rich
- Has been a radio host, a theater critic, and dramaturg
- Became creative director of the Jujamcyn Theaters as a result of a bad review he once gave *Big River*
- Was one of two lead producers of the Tony Kushner two-part opus *Angels in America* when it was on Broadway; the first installment, *Angels in America: Millennium Approaches*, opened on Broadway at the Walter Kerr Theatre on May 4, 1993 and closed on December 4, 1994, where it ran for 367 performances; the second installment, *Angels in America: Perestroika*, opened at the same theater on November 23, 1993 and closed on December 4, 1994, where it ran for 217 performances
- Produced the last six plays of August Wilson; the final one, *Radio Golf*, opened on Broadway at the Cort Theatre, on May 8, 2007 and closed July 1, 2007, running for 64 performances
- Currently serving as artistic director of Encores, which showcases obscure or forgotten American musicals

SECTION III
The Nonprofit Route

CHAPTER 6
Joseph Papp

b. June 22, 1921, Brooklyn, NY, USA – **d.** October 31, 1991, New York, NY, USA

"His ego was huge, but instead of slickness, he exuded reserve and a sobriety that made me think of Old Testament patriarchs. Some people he worked with found his seriousness almost unrelieved.... He was not a smiler and I always felt a sense of accomplishment after eliciting his laughter. I also felt free."

—Helen Epstein, from *Joe Papp: An American Life*

"He was a man of principle."

—Allison Harper, former Papp staffer

Joseph Papp circa 1972

The Crusader

Like other legends such as Florenz Ziegfeld, David Belasco, and David Merrick, Joseph Papp was larger than life—charismatic, dynamic, and imposing—a mythical figure in the making even during his lifetime. But as far as ideology went, Papp was the polar opposite.

First, he was never in it—meaning theater—for a buck. In fact, even when his beloved Public Theater (which he founded in 1967 in the old Astor Library building on Lafayette Street in Greenwich Village) was flourishing, sending homegrown productions like *A Chorus Line* or *Hair* to Broadway, Papp used its cumulative profits to subsidize noncommercial workshop productions or other ventures where money was as elusive as the Holy Grail. At the height of his success, Papp would not take a raise—though later he did after much persuasion.

Second, Papp, a child of impoverished immigrant parents, was an advocate of the underclass and disenfranchised minorities, feeling more affinity for them than for the socialites who would pour funds into Lincoln Center's Vivian Beaumont Theater, where he would—for a brief period, concurrent with his duties at the Public—act as co-artistic director. For several decades, Papp ruled the not-for-profit domain with his Public Theater, championing socially relevant, timely plays by then unknown scribes such as David Rabe and Thomas Babe, both of whom he would form surrogate father/son relationships with. He was the definition of a great man, but like many a great man, he was deeply flawed and a paradox (of which he was greatly aware).

Yet underneath the flash and flamboyance, Papp had the soul and sensibility of an altruist and an educator. His all-consuming, populist determination to present free Shakespeare in Central Park to individuals across the socioeconomic spectrum culminated in a victory (the first of many in a long and remarkable career) over parks commissioner Robert Moses. Born and bred in a tenement apartment in Williamsburg, Brooklyn, Papp is a true success story whose greatest legacies to the American theater are the institutions he created from the ground up, which endure to this day: the New York Shakespeare Festival and the Public Theater.

Falling in Love with the Bard

The seeds for Papp's lifelong love for Shakespeare were first sown in a class assignment when he was only twelve years old. His English teacher asked him and his fellow students to memorize and recite in class a speech from Shakespeare's *Julius Caesar*. Papp was transfixed by words spoken in iambic pentameter. He was hooked, and for the rest of his life he would be able to recite countless monologues from Shakespeare's plays without missing a beat.

Another formative moment in Papp's blossoming love affair with Shakespeare occurred in 1936, when his speech teacher took his class to two productions of *Hamlet* that were playing on Broadway. One starred the classically trained British stage actor John Gielgud (years before he became known to American audiences for his roles in popular movies such as *Arthur*), and the other starred the British film actor Leslie Howard, who had no classical training. Supposedly Papp liked how natural Leslie Howard sounded, but was irritated by what he considered to be Gielgud's pretentious, stilted diction. This aversion would lay the groundwork for Papp's disdain toward actors using mannered accents when playing Shakespeare. He hated that type of artificial theatrical diction, feeling that because people didn't speak that way at all in everyday life, why should they speak that way onstage and while performing Shakespeare, no less?

In November 1942, Papp joined the Navy and got some firsthand experience with what he would later be doing professionally in his life: He was put in charge of mounting variety shows on the ship. From his crewmates, he chose performers; he also did imitations, made up jokes, and served as emcee. In 1945, Papp was sent to California to create an entertainment unit similar to what the Army had (and still has). There he put together a more sophisticated troupe of singers and dancers (including an unknown named Bob Fosse) who would tour Honolulu, Guam, Japan, the Aleutian Islands, and Alaska.

Discharged from the Navy in August 1946, Papp enrolled in The Actor's Lab, a new theater school in Los Angeles, and paid no tuition courtesy of the G.I. Bill. The Lab was founded by esteemed members of the Group Theatre, who counted among their ranks Lee Strasberg, Harold Clurman, and Cheryl Crawford. They were committed to presenting plays that had resonating social or political value. Many Lab members were left-leaning and would later find themselves running afoul of the House Un-American Activities Committee during the Red Scare of the late 1940s and the 1950s. Since films were supplanting theater as steadier and far more lucrative employment, disgruntled Group members bolted for the West Coast. Dismayed by a creative community they deemed culturally arid, they formed The Actor's Lab as a way to counteract the philistinism and political apathy that prevailed around them.

Feeling a strong predilection for socialist doctrine as well as plays that were topically provocative, Papp reveled in his new learning environment. The one thing he could not abide, though, was the overemphasis on the Method, an acting technique that encourages actors to draw upon personal memories for emotionally laden scenes. Papp felt the Method diminished an actor's ability to play with language à la Shakespeare. Working with actors who ostensibly only cared about becoming movie stars and not about elocution was very frustrating to the future founder of the New York Shakespeare Festival.

In February 1948, Joe Bromberg, Rose Hobart, Roman Bohnen, and Will Lee, four senior members of the Lab, testified before the California branch of the House Un-American Activities Committee. They were asked if they had ever been members of the Communist Party; all refused to answer. As a result, their careers were over and the beginning of the end for the Lab was near. In May 1950, the Lab (now renamed the New Globe after the Lab filed for bankruptcy following the HUAC fallout) closed shop. Papp was without a creative home—at least for now.

It was a seminal experience for Papp, providing him with a thorough tutorial on how to run a nonprofit theater. Key lessons Papp learned from his time at the Lab (where in addition to being a student, he also acted as an office manager and janitor) were how to fundraise, how to attract and increase your audience base, how to solicit government agencies for money, and how to use the proceeds of productions to subsidize noncommercial work. These lessons would come in handy in no time.

Back in New York City

In early 1951, Papp moved back to New York City and took a part-time job as a floor manager for CBS. During this very lean period, Papp did some directing and teaching, but nothing of import happened until, according to Helen Epstein in her biography *Joe Papp: An American Life,* he worked one summer as a social director at a socialist camp in the Catskills and "persuaded an elderly, leftist Daughter of the American Revolution to give him money to start a theater. With $1,000, Joe turned a barn into a playhouse, paid three friends to come up to the Catskills, and produced a series of plays."

Later that same year, Papp became a full-time stage manager for CBS. It was the early days of the Golden Age of television. Though he disdained the medium, he did find it to be an excellent training ground and would often ask people in the know how certain shows were cast and produced.

He was also looking for directing jobs, and with Bernard Gersten, Charles Cooper, and Peter Lawrence—friends of his from the Lab days—he chipped in some money to produce a Sean O'Casey play, with Papp directing. What was interesting about this production, which was staged in the Yugoslav-American Hall in Hell's Kitchen, was that it established an important precedent for future Papp productions: interracial casting—a rarity in those days. Papp cast two African-American actors, in addition to Irish actors. The idea germinated when he was a student at the Lab and would hear older Lab members talk about casting more African-Americans in roles, without following up on it. For Papp, casting African-American actors as Irish characters wasn't a problem, as long as they could speak the brogue.

At this point, Papp met a person who would play a significant role in getting publicity for his shows as well as getting elusive, highbrow theater critics (like the venerable Brooks Atkinson from the *New York Times*) to see those shows: Merle Debuskey. Though Debuskey primarily worked the Broadway circuit, he loved O'Casey's plays and was impressed with the indefatigable Papp. Atkinson did attend a performance, although it's unclear whether Debuskey's efforts had anything to do with that coup. Unfortunately, the review was less than flattering. Papp was devastated and wondered if he should do something else. But theater was all he knew and wanted to do.

Unbeknownst to Papp, he had been under surveillance by the FBI since 1948 when he was at the Lab. Papp had been attending Communist Party meetings and associating with members, which the FBI had been tracking. By 1953, they had compiled a considerable file on him. Their spying would come to a head several years later, embroiling Papp in one of contemporary America's darkest chapters: McCarthyism.

In the meantime, the resilient Papp rebounded from the scathing Atkinson review to direct a production of *Deep Are the Roots*. Soon after, Papp looked for a venue to start his own theater. He chose a dilapidated room in an East Village church—Seymour Hall in Emmanuel Church, which Epstein describes as having "a shallow stage, no wings, no curtains over the windows or altar, and no division between the audience and actor." There he inaugurated his Shakespeare Workshop; admission to performances was free, but no one got paid for services rendered either—the actors would use this experience performing classical roles as a way to build up their résumés. Producing the oeuvre of an author who had been dead for hundreds of years did have a decided advantage: Papp didn't have to pay him royalties.

Presenting Free Shakespeare

The next step Papp took to transform his dream into reality was applying to the New York State Department of Education for a charter, which was rarely granted to theaters. Submitting a mission statement where he outlined the educational importance of the workshop, Papp was soon granted a charter from the New York State Board of Regents. After spending evenings and weekends sprucing up Seymour Hall, Papp went to work finding actors and directors for his initial Shakespearean productions.

Unfortunately, he had little success finding a director for *Romeo and Juliet,* so he ended up directing it himself. Compounding the problems was the attrition rate for the actors: Many quit soon after being cast. Finding this untenable, Papp wisely postponed *Romeo and Juliet* to make way for an evening of scenes culled from Shakespeare's plays. It opened on November 4,

1954—and thus commenced over five decades of Joseph Papp's mission to present free Shakespeare to New Yorkers.

Several months later, in February, Papp (who by now had shortened his surname from Papirofsky to Papp) presented "An Evening with Shakespeare's Women," which featured scenes and ended with a lecture by a college professor. A then unknown actress named Colleen Dewhurst appeared in this performance, acting a scene from *Henry V.* The audience was almost full to capacity, but paying for expenses was a struggle. Yet Papp had a far-reaching vision that transcended the immediate pursuit of money. He dreamed of establishing a theater that would be different from Broadway or even off-Broadway, one where "there were no assigned seats, no ticket-takers, no admissions fee—just green lawns. ..."[1]

Soon he set his sights on the East River amphitheater, and on August 3, 1956, the newly christened New York Shakespeare Festival opened with a production of *The Taming of the Shrew* starring Colleen Dewhurst, Roscoe Lee Browne, and Jacob Cannon. Papp had begun actively courting critics, especially those from the *New York Times,* to attend the production. Though the dean of critics, Atkinson, did not attend the early performances, Arthur Gelb, a second-string critic from the *Times,* did. During the intermission, the skies opened up, unleashing a downpour, which prevented the show from continuing. Gelb wrote in the paper positively and with heartfelt sentiment about the experience and what Papp was trying to accomplish.

The article drew a lot of attention and support from both the theatrical community and New York residents. The crowds clamored for seats, and even the elusive Atkinson finally attended a performance. He wrote a rave, praising the performances of the lead actors and imploring readers to give money to the festival.

Going Mobile

Soon Papp tired of the East River amphitheater and wanted to move his burgeoning enterprise into Central Park; he also wanted to bring free Shakespeare to all five boroughs. To accommodate the latter goal, a 35-foot trailer truck with a mobile stage was designed. Papp also contacted a city official, Deputy Mayor Stanley Lowell. And thanks to Lowell's intercession and Papp's powers of persuasion, the city "contributed the equivalent of $15,000 to $20,000 in manpower and equipment toward his mobile theater."[2]

With forty actors and artistic director Stuart Vaughan in tow, Papp and his troupe toured the boroughs during the 1957 summer season with *Romeo and Juliet, Two Gentleman of Verona,* and *Macbeth.* The mobile theater soon garnered attention from the press, with reporters hot on the heels of Papp's group as they performed throughout New York City proper. As the tour began in Central Park, it ended up in that same destination, baptizing its run there with *Romeo and Juliet,* with the other two plays to follow. All elicited rave reviews.

The following year, Papp's attempts to solicit funding from the New York City Board of Education came to naught. But Papp was determined, and anything that stood in his way of fulfilling his populist raison d'être was just a temporary setback. The big problem Papp faced from bureaucrats, such as Mayor Wagner and Park Commissioner Robert Moses, was caused by his adamant refusal to charge theatergoers an admissions fee. Both Wagner and Moses wanted Papp to charge money for tickets because if he did, it meant the city would be reimbursed for donating money and equipment to the Festival as well as a precious section of Central Park. Only Papp didn't see it that way. He felt the city should embrace wholeheartedly, and without expecting any remuneration, what he was trying to do—and that was bring the timeless beauty of the Bard's words to several generations of theatergoers who would normally not be able to afford Broadway or even off-Broadway, but who could go see one of Papp's Shakespearean productions because it was accessible and free.

Rearing Its Ugly Head

While Papp was fighting for his dream, his past came back to bite him in a big way: He was subpoenaed to testify before the House Un-American Activities Committee. When asked if he had ever "been a member of the Communist Party," Papp refused to answer, invoking the Fifth Amendment, which protects individuals against self-incrimination. Afterward, he was fired by CBS. Papp told the network he would fight them. And sure enough, the supernova from Williamsburg won his case. CBS was ordered to reinstate Papp, stating that his dismissal had been without grounds and cause. But Papp was never one to be predictable. Several months after his reinstatement, he left his job at CBS. He decided to devote himself full-time to the festival.

What ensued was one of the most difficult—and fulfilling—chapters of Papp's ascending career: the establishment of the New York Shakespeare Festival's Central Park venue, the Delacorte Theater. But like many things in Papp's life, he didn't get it without a fight. To get Central Park, he had to go through the immutable colossus known as Robert Moses. In early 1959, Moses rejected Papp's application for a summer performance permit in Central Park, citing issues such as "considerable park acreage ... being damaged by your operation," as well as "no sanitary or dressing facilities" for the actors. Continuing in this vein, Moses wrote, "The cost of the work the City must do if your Shakespeare in Central Park is to continue is between

$100,000 and $150,000. If your performances are worthwhile, people will pay a reasonable charge to see them. . . ."[3] The city would not issue Papp a permit unless he agreed to charge admissions to theatergoers and enter into a "concession agreement" in which "10 percent of the gross receipts" would go to the Department of Parks & Recreation. Such an ultimatum was anathema to Papp's purpose in presenting free Shakespeare in the Park. He sued Moses, arguably the most influential public official serving the City of New York at that time—and won.

Respecting Papp's unyielding resolve, Moses requisitioned money from the city's coffers to build an amphitheater in Central Park for Papp's New York Shakespeare Festival. The theater, built in 1961, was named after George T. Delacorte, an early patron of the Shakespeare Workshop and mobile theater. It debuted with *The Merchant of Venice*, starring George C. Scott and James Earl Jones, during the summer of 1962.

Since then, Shakespeare in the Park has become an annual summer staple, attracting crowds and employing top-of-the-line actors like Meryl Streep, who began her career following her graduation from the Yale School of Drama in the mid-1970s with the festival. (She returned in 2001 with a production of *The Seagull*, and in 2006 with *Mother Courage*, both of which drew tepid reviews but record-breaking attendance.)

Productions at the Delacorte have also gone on to Broadway, including *The Mystery of Edwin Drood*, which opened on December 2, 1985, at the Imperial Theatre and ran for 608 performances, winning Tonys for Best Musical, Best Book, and Original Score (Rupert Holmes), Best Actor (George Rose), and Best Direction of a Musical (Wilford Leach); and *The Tempest*, which opened November 1, 1995 (four years after Papp's death), and had a far less successful stint, running for only 70 performances.

Finding a Home

Following his triumph over Moses, Papp searched for a venue that would act as the year-round artistic haven for his populist theater. He found it in the former Astor Library in the East Village. The landmark building had first opened to the public in 1854, several years after the death of the financier John Jacob Astor, who wanted to create a great library for the city. Eventually the building was sold to the Hebrew Immigrant Aid Society, which used it as a way station for incoming immigrants. Then, in 1965, it was sold to a developer who wanted to demolish it. The Landmarks Preservation Commission stepped in and paved the way for Papp to purchase it for $560,000. In early 1966, Papp publicly announced the acquisition, ushering in yet another new chapter in his extraordinary career.

The inaugural production for Papp's Public Theater was another mile-stone: the world premiere of *Hair*. With music by Galt McDermot and lyrics and book by James Rado and Gerome Ragni, *Hair* was one of the most successful shows to have started at the Public Theater before relocating uptown to the Main Stem (the other being *A Chorus Line*). A loosely structured rock musical that dealt with free love, hippies, the Vietnam War, and other burning issues of the day pertinent to young people, *Hair* was unlike anything that had ever been seen before by theatergoers. Opening at the Public on October 17, 1967, it became a sensation and later moved to Broadway's Biltmore Theater, where it played for 1,873 performances.

During this time, Papp, who began to teach directing at the Yale School of Drama at the invitation of Dean Robert Brustein, continued to seek out original plays that were topical, provocative, and cutting-edge, such as Charles Gordone's *No Place to Be Somebody*, the first play by an African-American playwright to win the Pulitzer Prize. Papp gravitated toward plays that reflected the social and political maelstrom in which contemporary society had plunged in the late 1960s: an unpopular war in Vietnam was raging on; Robert F. Kennedy and Dr. Martin Luther King, Jr., two beacons of hope for the future, had been cut down by assassins' bullets; and the hippie counterculture was exhorting disaffected youths to "tune in and drop out," widening the already gaping divide between them and their elders, or the "Establishment." By now Papp was middle-aged, and though he would not cultivate the demeanor and flower-power patter of the younger generation, he very much wanted his beloved Public Theater to mirror all that was going on in the nation. He wanted his theater to deal with a dimension of experiences that went beyond the limited compass of the upper-crust white Anglo elite. He wanted his artistic universe to be ecumenical, folding in a diversity of ethnicities and creeds.

Man of Principle

It was Papp's pronounced social conscience that first attracted Allison Harper's attention. A staffer at the Repertory Theater of Lincoln Center, Harper first became aware of Papp in the summer of 1960 while attending a Shakespeare in the Park production of *Henry V*. She noted that James Earl Jones, the African-American actor who would later become well known for his distinctive baritone and noble bearing, was playing Williams, a role nor-mally played by a white actor. This interracial casting intrigued and impressed her, especially because it was an anomaly at that time.

After she quit her job at Lincoln Center, Harper contacted Papp, and in February 1967, she went to work for him for that upcoming season of

Shakespeare in the Park, where she was in charge of subscriptions.
That summer, Papp asked Harper if she would stay on because he would be
launching his Public Theater that fall with *Hair*. Harper agreed and worked
for Papp until he died.

As an employer and producer, she found him exemplary. "I think he was
a very clever marketer," she recalls. "Also, he was a very benevolent dictator as
far as running his staff was concerned. He was wonderful—and available—to
us. He looked after us so that we were paid the best he could pay us. Later,
when things like health insurance weren't dreams in people's eyes, he really
saw that we got it. He set up things like that— that protected us."

When asked what she feels his most significant contribution to American
theater was, Harper proffers up a startling, though not surprising, tidbit:
"Just being a sterling example of a socially conscious man and sticking to
his guns—not taking tainted money. When Phillip Morris wanted to give
us money, he said no because of the cancer issue." Papp's commitment to
rectifying social injustice was such that even when he was terminally ill with
prostate cancer, he still protested as censorship the National Endowment of
the Arts cutting off funds in 1990 to performance artists Karen Finley, Tim
Miller, John Fleck, and Holly Hughes.

From Workshop to Classic

After *Hair*, the next benchmark achievement for Joe Papp and the Public
Theater was *A Chorus Line*. Because so much of what transpired artistically
at the Public happened within the protected sanctum of workshops, some of
which never saw the light of day, there was a lot of artistic experimentation
going on in the former Astor Library. In the early 1970s, a former Broadway
dancer turned choreographer, Michael Bennett, had an idea about creating a
show based on the real-life experiences of "gypsies"—anonymous Broadway
chorus dancers who migrate from show to show, never moving into the spot-
light to become stars. Bennett wanted to lead a workshop where he would
audiotape the personal feelings these gypsies had about their backgrounds,
lives, and careers. What resulted was a musical, featuring a score by Marvin
Hamlisch, lyrics by Edward Kleban, book by James Kirkwood and Nicholas
Dante, and direction/choreography by Bennett; several of the workshop
participants in the original cast would go on to Broadway.

Opening in May 1975 at the Public Theater, *A Chorus Line* received
glowing reviews across the board and, two months later, moved uptown to
the Shubert Theater, where it became a critical and commercial phenomenon.
It would play there for fifteen years, becoming one of Broadway's longest-
running musicals (surpassed only by *Cats* and *Phantom of the Opera*). The
following year, it would win nine Tony Awards, including Best Musical,

Best Direction, Best Original Score, and Best Book; it would also receive the Pulitzer Prize. Proceeds from *A Chorus Line* provided an endless stream of revenue for Papp to sponsor a multitude of noncommercial productions and workshops. It gave him the freedom to care even less than he did before about staging shows to generate profit.

On Papp, Stuart W. Little wrote in his 1972 book *Off Broadway:* "He was blithely uninterested in money except for the result it could produce. ... He dealt in immense sums, but money was meaningless to him until it was translated into what he alone valued, into theater."

From 1973 to 1977, Papp's New York Shakespeare Festival, extending beyond the parameters of downtown Manhattan and Central Park, took up residence at the Vivian Beaumont Theater, previously the home base of the Repertory Theater of Lincoln Center. On Papp's dual duties at Lincoln Center, Stuart W. Little wrote in his 1974 book *Enter Joseph Papp:* "He wanted the Beaumont because it would buttress his commitment to dramatic material that dealt with the major social themes of the time. He wanted the Beaumont because its already large subscription audience could be expanded and reconstituted, democratized, made more nearly consonant with the social purpose he had espoused. ... He wanted the Beaumont precisely because he was in poor financial shape at the Public. Escalate or perish. If in this month of March 1973 Papp had some need of the Beaumont, Lincoln Center had even more need of Joseph Papp."

Among the shows produced there under Papp's vigilant watch were David Rabe's *In the Boom Boom Room* and *Streamers,* as well as revivals such as *Hamlet,* starring Sam Waterston, and *The Threepenny Opera*, with Raul Julia. Though Papp did succeed in upping box-office receipts to near $4 million for the Beaumont, he never felt comfortable working uptown in the posher, more conservative Lincoln Center. "I feel I cannot grow at Lincoln Center," said Papp at the time. "It's a showcase, not a place where things develop."[4] After four years, Papp happily returned to his downtown creative domicile full-time.

A Frightening Disease Descends

In addition to fostering and promoting new playwrights, Papp always took several young, up-and-coming actors under his paternal wing. They included Meryl Streep, Kevin Kline—who started off as a spear-carrier in Shakespeare in the Park before moving up into larger roles—and Mandy Patinkin, who bonded with Papp over their Jewish heritage, even celebrating holidays together. All would find their careers ineradicably shaped and immeasurably enhanced by their appearances at both Shakespeare in the Park and the Public Theater. And all would develop a longstanding friendship with their mentor,

Papp. (Kline and his wife, Phoebe Cates, gave one of their children the middle name of Joseph in homage to Papp.)

Kline would star as the Pirate King in the next successful production for Papp: a new production of Gilbert and Sullivan's operetta *The Pirates of Penzance*. Staged in the summer of 1980 at the Delacorte Theater, *Penzance,* which also starred Linda Ronstadt, Rex Smith, George Rose, and Estelle Parsons, fared so well with critics and the audience that it later transferred to Broadway, opening January 21, 1981. It would run for 787 performances and play at the Uris and Minskoff theaters. The show would net yet another Tony for Papp for Best Revival, as well as trophies for Papp stalwart and friend Wilford Leach (Best Direction), and Kline for Best Actor in a Musical.

In the early 1980s, Papp's professional achievements were at an apex: The Public Theater and New York Shakespeare Festival were thriving, their cachet built from their history, their mission, and the unflagging efforts of überpromoter/impresario Joseph Papp. But an unknown and frightening pestilence was starting to surface, decimating sizable chunks of the theater community. In its early days, it was given the ominous moniker "gay cancer," by virtue of the fact that homosexual men were prominently susceptible victims; later it would become known by mainstream society as AIDS. Papp would feel firsthand its devastating effects, from members of his inner circle (his beloved colleague and friend Wilford Leach) to his own family (his adored son Tony, who died of the disease months before Papp succumbed to prostate cancer).

After much editing and rewriting by Gail Merrifield, Papp's fourth wife, who headed the Public's play development department, the Public produced Larry Kramer's *The Normal Heart,* about bureaucratic indifference to the AIDS crisis in the early 1980s, in 1985. After being rejected by nearly every agent in town, *The Normal Heart* emerged as one of the first important plays to deal with AIDS.

The Final Stage

After Papp was diagnosed with prostate cancer in the late 1980s, he started to court a number of individuals, such as the multiple Tony Award–winning director Jerry Zaks and even Meryl Streep, to be his successor. Though both were immensely flattered, they declined the offer. Eventually, he handpicked avant-garde director JoAnne Akalaitis to assume the reins after him. (Akalaitis's reign as artistic director of the Public Theater following Papp's death on October 31, 1991, would last only twenty months; she would be replaced by George C. Wolfe, who led the Public for thirteen years before stepping down.)

Though battling a terminal illness, which he kept hidden from many save his closest friends and colleagues, Papp still had the characteristic fire smoldering in his belly. In April 1990, he refused to sign an anti-obscenity agreement from the National Endowment of the Arts in order to receive a $50,000 grant. He would soon publicly claim that as a result of this refusal, he had received pledges of gifts totaling more than $60,000. Even with his health seriously in decline, Papp remained very much a man who tenaciously stuck to his principles.

A bold visionary and iconoclast who was never afraid to oppose the big guns that might crush his dreams, Papp remains, in memory and influence, an industry behemoth, forever enshrined in the pantheon of American theater. Walk into the Public Theater, still a foremost presenter of original, cutting-edge work, or check out a show at the Delacorte Theater, which recently celebrated the fiftieth anniversary of its free Shakespeare in the Park productions, and you'll feel the weight of his once omnipotent presence permeating the air.

Career Highlights

- Won a legal battle in 1957 with then Parks Commissioner Robert Moses to establish an annual summer theater to present free Shakespeare in Central Park
- Founded the Public Theater in 1967 in the old Astor Library in downtown Manhattan
- Inaugurated his Public Theater with *Hair* in 1967; the show became so successful it quickly moved to Broadway, making it the first off-Broadway musical to undergo that transition
- Produced the classic musical *A Chorus Line* in 1975, which began life as a workshop at the Public Theater; like *Hair,* the original production quickly moved to Broadway where it would be one of the longest running shows in Broadway history
- Produced Charles Gordone's *No Place to Be Somebody* at the Public; Gordone was the first black playwright to win the Pulitzer Prize
- Introduced playwrights such as David Rabe, Jason Miller, and Thomas Babe to off-Broadway and the American theater
- Acted as mentor to Oscar-winning actors Meryl Streep and Kevin Kline when they first began their stage careers
- Though terminally ill with prostate cancer, became a vocal opponent to censorship after the National Endowment of the Arts withheld funds to four controversial performance artists in 1990

End Notes

1. From Helen Epstein's *Joe Papp: An American Life.*
2. From *Joe Papp: An American Life.*
3. From *Joe Papp: An American Life.*
4. From *Time* Magazine, "Papp's Curtain at Lincoln Center," June 20, 1977.

CHAPTER 7
Andre Bishop

"He supports the writers like gangbusters and has the most integrity of any person I know."

—William Ivey Long, multiple Tony Award–winning costume designer

Andre Bishop

Nonprofit Guru

For over thirty-five years, nonprofit off-Broadway theaters have nurtured and promoted provocative new works penned by gifted—and unknown—playwrights who would never have come into prominence if these creative havens hadn't been accessible to noncommercial talent. Artists such as the late playwright Wendy Wasserstein (*The Heidi Chronicles*), Christopher Durang (*Sister Mary Ignatius Explains It All for You*), and musical composer/lyricist William Finn (*March of the Falsettos*) owe the launch of their highly prolific careers to one particular off-Broadway nonprofit theater, Playwrights Horizons, which, since its founding in 1971 by Robert Moss, has been invested with an express mission to develop and support new work. The galvanizing agent that helped vault these artists into public view was not so much an institution or an abstract philosophy, but a flesh-and-blood man who served as artistic director of Playwrights Horizons from 1981 to 1991: Andre Bishop. Currently Bishop rules the Lincoln Center theater realm in the same role, a post he's held since early 1992, when he replaced Gregory Mosher. What makes Bishop a necessary and significant addition on our list is that he has produced hundreds of new plays and musicals under the nonprofit banner, many of which have earned top prizes from critics and box-office-breaking approval from discerning theatergoers.

Though Bishop has not had to wrestle with a spate of problems (mostly financial) that periodically plague some of our illustrious commercial producers, he has had to deal with his ample share of angst. Imbued with immoderate poise, oratory eloquence, and a disarmingly gentle manner, it's all in a day's work for the Harvard-educated Bishop.

The Salad Days

Growing up in New York City, Bishop attended a lot of Broadway shows as a child and knew his future calling was in the theater. Thus his theater journey was initiated with a familiar step: He tried to be an actor. After studying acting in college and later for a brief spell at the Neighborhood Playhouse, Bishop took classes with renowned acting coach Wynn Handman, the artistic director and cofounder of the American Place Theatre, and pursued a career with mixed results. Though Bishop landed roles at the American Place Theatre and some voiceovers, he felt frustrated and lost.

"I think I was reasonably talented in a sort of quirky way," he recalls when discussing his early stab at acting, "but I just lacked the confidence somehow, not when I got onstage. But getting onstage—the auditioning and all that—I just didn't have the confidence or perhaps the right ego for acting."

Paul Kolnik

Ethan Hawke and Billy Crudup in a scene from the Lincoln Center Theater production of *Voyage*, part one of Tom Stoppard's trilogy *The Coast of Utopia*

Bishop, who was in his mid-twenties at the time, contacted a college friend of his, who was directing shows at a rising off-Broadway theater company called Playwrights Horizons. He told his friend that he was feeling "unmoored" and wanted to work in theater, "but I don't know if I can be an actor." His college chum introduced Bishop to Robert Moss, then head of Playwrights Horizons. The meeting, which took place in 1975, would prove to be productive for Bishop and put him on the track to becoming one of New York theater's foremost not-for-profit theater producers.

A New Venture

"Bob Moss was a very cheerful kind of man," recounts the cerebral and vaguely avuncular Bishop, in his cramped Lincoln Center office, whose walls are adorned with posters of past shows. "[He said to me,] 'What do you want to do?' I said, 'I don't know. Let me just kind of hang out.' So I did. I answered the phones, sharpened pencils. This was at a time when Playwrights Horizons and the nonprofit movement in general were very small—very fledgling. What happened was that I found the mission of Playwrights Horizons, which was to nurture and develop and produce new American playwrights, very exciting. It was a cause I could easily believe in because one has to understand that in the mid-1970s, there were very few nonprofit theaters devoted to doing new plays, unlike today. The Broadway theater was growing inhospitable to new works, especially new works by unknown playwrights. The theater in New York City then was in transition. Certainly, [that was the case with] the regional theater movement that was very much beginning by the 1970s. But new plays were not on their agenda. Nowadays yes, but not then."

Later, after Bishop began working at Playwrights Horizons, the company relocated to its present-day digs on 42nd Street, paving the way for other theaters to follow suit (hence the moniker "Theater Row" for that area). Bishop found the humble, ungentrified surroundings to be both "a nightmare and exhilarating." Soon he became a literary manager by default.

"I was among the first literary managers in New York—and in the country. I read plays, wrote reports, and eventually started producing in the smaller studio theater. Then times got very tough at Playwrights Horizons. It was about ten years old. Bob Moss had just had it. It was just too difficult. In those days, it was much cheaper to live in New York than it is now—luckily." Faced with mountainous debt, Moss told Bishop he had two options: close Playwrights Horizons or have Bishop take over and "do with it what you will." The latter proposition floored Bishop not just for its generosity but because it was emanating from the founder of Playwrights Horizons.

"I had made myself what I wanted to be—indispensable," relates Bishop. "I thought about [the offer] for not a very long time and decided to keep on going. Playwrights Horizons went on to produce a number of playwrights with whom I felt a kinship. We started doing musicals there. And we had a number of hits in a row—A.R. Gurney's *The Dining Room,* Christopher Durang's *Sister Mary,* William Finn's *March of the Falsettos*—and suddenly Playwrights Horizons was a going concern again. Thank God. That's how I started. What I always say to students is, I was very lucky because I had no training. I happened to walk into a theater and a theater movement (i.e., the nonprofit theater movement) that was about at the same stage of life experience as I was. As Playwrights Horizons and as indeed the nonprofit theater grew, so did I. I was kind of the right person at the right time. I had no idea I'd end up being an artistic director of a theater."

Becoming an Artistic Director

Bishop's first producing project as artistic director of Playwrights Horizons was William Finn's *March of the Falsettos.* Bishop got involved with the project because he had known Finn for a while—Playwrights had previously mounted a musical of his called *In Trousers.* Bishop attended presentations of *Falsetto* (a sequel to *In Trousers,* about the story of Marvin, his ex-wife Trina, son Jason, gay lover Whizzer, and psychiatrist Mendel) in its early incarnations in Finn's living room. Because *Falsettos* was staged by a nonprofit theater, meaning a noncommercial one funded by grants, donors, and a growing subscription audience, Bishop balks at quoting a ballpark figure of how much *Falsettos* cost. It was over twenty-five years ago, when budgets were considerably lower, unions were far fewer, and the contract that Playwrights worked on was not so conducive to an actor's income.

"Things just didn't cost very much then," says Bishop. "Also, *Falsettos* opened initially in a seventy-five-seat studio theater upstairs. Actors and artists in general got paid very little. What I always say is that with these plays and musicals at these nonprofit theaters years ago, it wasn't so much the donors or the funding sources that subsidized the shows; it was the artists, because they worked for so little." After opening at Playwrights on May 20, 1981, and closing four months later on September 26, *March of the Falsettos*, directed by James Lapine (and produced by Playwrights Horizons) re-opened for an off-Broadway commercial engagement on October 13 that same year, at the Westside Theatre. It closed on January 31, 1982, after running for 268 performances.

At Playwrights Horizons, Bishop produced notable productions that included Wendy Wasserstein's *The Heidi Chronicles,* Alfred Uhry's *Driving Miss Daisy,* and the Stephen Sondheim/James Lapine musical *Sunday in the*

Paul Kolnik

Amy Irving and Jennifer Ehle in *Shipwreck*, part two of *The Coast of Utopia*

Park with George. All would win Pulitzer Prizes for their respective authors, with *The Heidi Chronicles* and *Sunday in the Park with George* moving to success-ful Broadway runs; and *Driving Miss Daisy* moving to the big screen in 1989, where it would snag Oscars for Best Picture and Best Actress (Jessica Tandy).

Also, while at Playwrights, Bishop had been showered with numerous laurels, among them the 1983 Margo Jones Award for contributions made to the American theater; the 1989 Lucille Lortel Award for Outstanding Body of Work, specifically in the development of new American plays and play-wrights; and a special Drama Desk Award in 1992. In 1991, Bishop seemed to be at the pinnacle of a career that he had never imagined. He loved his job and his staff, and he was proud of what he had accomplished at Playwrights Horizons. He never thought he would ever leave, but much to his surprise, a bigger opportunity awaited—one that would truly test and challenge his artistic judgment and administrative mettle: artistic director of Lincoln Center Theater. And Bishop didn't even have to campaign for it.

A New Challenge Beckons

"I got the job without having to do anything. I got a call from Bernie Gersten [executive producer of Lincoln Center Theater], whom I knew because I had worked for him at the Delacorte Theater during the summer of 1971 and then kept up a friendship with him off and on. At one point, before he came [to Lincoln Center Theater], he was going to work for Playwrights Horizons. We were talking with him about that. Then he called me up and said that [then artistic director of Lincoln Center Theater] Gregory Mosher was leaving and asked me if I had any ideas of people who might be good replacements."

Gersten previously approached Bishop for artistic director suggestions in the mid-1980s after the two venues that constitute Lincoln Center Theater—the Broadway-eligible Vivian Beaumont Theater and the off-Broadway Mitzi E. Newhouse Theater—reopened. Bishop told Gersten that a director needed to be the creative head in order to overcome the difficulties inherent to stag-ing a production in the Beaumont's thrust space. His advice was duly taken and in 1985, former New York City Mayor John V. Lindsay asked Gregory Mosher, a Chicago-based director, to become artistic director of the newly established Lincoln Center Theater.

During a twenty-year period starting in the early 1960s, efforts had been made to revitalize theater at Lincoln Center, first under the stewardship of Elia Kazan, with his Repertory Theater of Lincoln Center and later with Joseph Papp. Unfortunately, theater at Lincoln Center mostly floundered instead of flourished. At the time of Mosher's accession to his post, a play had not been produced at either the Mitzi Newhouse or the Vivian Beaumont in four years. When Mosher took over, he aggressively pursued a younger and more diverse audience and programmed a full season of classics and new works by eminent playwrights (i.e., Tennessee Williams, Samuel Beckett), while also working with gifted unknowns, such as director/designer Julie Taymor. Within two years, the two theaters at Lincoln Center were jam-packed with delighted theatergoers and the annual income mushroomed to nearly $45 million. Such was the fiscal and artistic health of Lincoln Center Theater when Gersten phoned Bishop following Mosher's decision to leave his position.

"We went through a list," remembers Bishop. "I said, 'Yes, he would be good, she would be good, or this one wouldn't be good.' Finally, Bernie said, 'What would you think of Andre Bishop?' I was completely surprised because of what I had been doing at Playwrights Horizons. The mission of Playwrights Horizons is completely different from Lincoln Center Theater. I remember pausing and saying, 'Well, he might be interested'— because I was. Then Gregory called me. You have to understand, because I'm not tooting my own horn at all: In those days, which were the early 1990s, I was sort of the golden boy of the nonprofit theater, Playwrights Horizons. I think I was respected. I had worked hard.

"I never thought I would leave Playwrights Horizons at that point. I never thought I wanted to because in those days, Playwrights Horizons had meant everything to me. We had come from this tiny little theater into this extraordinary institution. I couldn't imagine my life without it. I was young when I came to Lincoln Center Theater in 1991. I was forty-two, forty-one years old. I didn't think about it very long when they offered me the job. I didn't interview and I knew, even though I would be torn apart by leaving Playwrights Horizons and would upset a lot of people there too, that this was a chance, because I didn't want to spend my entire career at Playwrights Horizons. Also, I was interested in doing old plays, classic plays in larger-scale productions, and I felt if I was lucky enough to get this job, even though it would be painful and wrenching because in many ways I was unprepared, I should take it."

A Precarious Start

Bishop had entertained fantasies of running the Public Theater because its mission seemed to mirror what he had been doing at Playwrights Horizons. But Bishop was realistic too, and knew he'd never get the opportunity to helm the Public because "I was probably considered too mainstream or white-bread." So he took the Lincoln Center job "with great pleasure and great trepidation."

Things became rocky right away. Bishop began his new job in January 1992, the middle of the season. "There was nothing in preparation here," sighs Bishop, remembering a very fraught period of transition for him. "Thank God I didn't know what I was getting myself in for, because I never would have taken the job."

Compounding his freshman difficulty with a new, wide-ranging, more high-profile job was having to adjust to new expenses, which were immeasurably higher than those incurred at Playwrights Horizons. "Bernie kept saying, 'Don't worry. It's the same thing—just more zeros,'" says Bishop. "I would say, 'Yes, but it's those zeros that worry me!'"

But not all was dour for Bishop. He had tremendous support from Gersten, as well as the board. Bishop was also able to bring to Lincoln Center Theater some key staffers from his tenure at Playwrights Horizons, which included erstwhile musical theater program director Ira Weitzman, casting director Daniel Swee, and Bishop's assistant Julia.

Still, Bishop instinctively knew that the real make-or-break obstacles he would have to conquer were Lincoln Center Theater's two spaces: the 1,060-seat Vivian Beaumont Theater and the 299-seat Mitzi E. Newhouse Theater. Where Playwrights Horizons' mainstage was a manageable 200-seat proscenium, Bishop now had to shoulder the onus of overseeing two venues that had been disparaged by many as "unworkable."

According to Bishop, what rendered these stages so problematic were their terrible acoustics and sightlines, both of which had been fixed in an $8 million renovation in 1996. Also, both theaters were thrust spaces, a configuration that can still be trying for theater artists.

"Years before the current administration, very few directors and designers knew how to use thrust stages. Now many do because they're all over the country. But in the late 1960s, when the Beaumont was built, they didn't know how to use it. So the theater was ahead of its time in some ways. And believe me, it still is a difficult space. It's not a space for kids to figure out how to direct. The Mitzi Newhouse is a thrust as well, but it's more intimate."

Bishop's criteria for choosing projects to be produced at the Lincoln Center Theater are predicated on his own taste and gut instinct as well as demands imposed by the two venues.

"What I respond to are often plays of language, plays of theatricality. But I'm also very interested in doing new American musicals. We've done a lot of them, which are rather serious and operalike as opposed to comedic. That said, I always have to keep in mind the two spaces here, which people now take for granted because we've done well and they come to all of our shows.

Not every play is right for the Beaumont Theater. Farces are not. Small, naturalistic Americana plays are not.

"I don't consider the Beaumont to be a theater for most new works. It's too big and too public; it's a Broadway theater. The Mitzi Newhouse is a writers' theater—everything in there seems kind of lovely. The Beaumont is a directors' theater." Because of this, Bishop often has to seriously ponder who will direct a project earmarked for that space.

Art over Commerce

Though the Beaumont may be a Broadway house, albeit the only one not located in the fabled Theater District, Bishop never considers the commercial possibilities of shows when programming for that theater. It just doesn't figure into his mindset; besides, it's a nonprofit theater and Lincoln Center Theater enjoys a huge and loyal subscription audience, he says. Luckily, he has not experienced problems with donors and board members over certain less-than-well-received productions, although he's sure that quite a few of them have disliked specific projects.

Bishop feels his most challenging project by far at Lincoln Center Theater has been one of his most successful ones: the recent marathon mounting in the Beaumont of Tom Stoppard's trilogy *The Coast of Utopia*, which tracks the lives of a group of Russian revolutionary thinkers and intellectuals from youth to middle age in the mid-19th century. In addition to breaking box-office records, the three plays that constitute the mammoth opus—*Voyage, Shipwreck,* and *Salvage*—generated mostly favorable reviews and snared the Tony Award for Best Play in June 2007. The plays were performed in repertory or on a rotating basis, the first time ever in the annals of Lincoln Center Theater history. (Although the Beaumont had begun life decades earlier as the Repertory Theater of Lincoln Center, this was a misnomer because there was no repertory.)

"*The Coast of Utopia* was probably the biggest challenge on every level that we've ever done. The cost of it, the scheduling of it, the juggling of forty-five actors, opening three parts of extremely difficult plays are extremely tough, as well as the sheer size of the scenery and the costumes, which are huge. Just the entire logistics of the marathon and the selling of the tickets—everything. This is not like doing *Damn Yankees, She Loves Me,* or *My Fair Lady.*"

The Coast of Utopia materialized because of Lincoln Center Theater's past history with staging Stoppard's plays (i.e., *Hapgood, Arcadia, The Invention of Love*). Bishop feels a strong commitment to Stoppard; he also wouldn't have staged *The Coast of Utopia* had director Jack O'Brien and designer Bob Crowley (both of whom would win Tonys for their respective work) not gotten involved with the project.

Producing for Broadway

During the 2005–06 season, Lincoln Center Theater produced the Broadway revival of Clifford Odets's *Awake and Sing*, which later garnered the Tony for Best Revival. The production, which opened on April 17, 2006, at the Belasco Theatre, and ran for a limited engagement ending on June 25, 2006, elicited glowing notices and enthusiastic audiences. What makes Bishop want to produce on Broadway—outside of the Beaumont, that is?

His response is clear-cut and frank: "When the Beaumont is occupied [is when I want to produce on Broadway]. Because it's the same contract, it's the same expense for us. Often if plays are successful at the Beaumont, we'll keep them running partly because they're too difficult and expensive to move if they do well, and partly because they're so directed and designed for a thrust stage. [If we move it] we'll have to completely redo them. Also, this allows me to pick plays that I can't normally do. Proscenium plays like *Awake and Sing* or *The Heiress* or *The Delicate Balance* would not have worked well in a thrust space. That's what's so great about Broadway. It's not because I think they're going to be commercial—it's the same membership, the same costs, and the same length of run."

Initially, the hardest part of Bishop's job was getting used to its demands and overcoming his fear of it. "I know that sounds crazy," he admits, "but I was very frightened and nervous for about the first five or six years here. Probably irrationally so. I thought if I had a disaster here I was going to be fired; I was in a state. The thing that frightens me the most is either not finding enough good new plays that we can do or when a show doesn't work out. But that doesn't frighten me, it disappoints me."

Voicing sentiments expressed by our other producers, Bishop gets terribly disheartened when a project that he intuitively feels—and knows—is good doesn't catch on or isn't well received by the press. Although the 2005 Lincoln Center Theater production of *The Light in the Piazza*, with music and lyrics by Adam Guettel and book by Craig Lucas, would go on to win several Tonys, one for Best Musical and another for Best Score, the show was hardly a success in its early stages. "It was everything I loved about new, serious musical theater," says Bishop, "and initially after we opened, it really didn't do that well critically. Most serious new musicals don't because it's very hard for critics to hear a score of complexity in one ear." *The Light in the Piazza* opened at the Beaumont on April 18, 2005, and closed on July 2, 2006; it ran for 504 performances.

Calling All Seasoned Talent

Unlike Playwrights Horizons, Lincoln Center Theater does not develop artists. According to Bishop, it would be closed in a year if that were its mission. What Lincoln Center does do is give opportunities to artists to exercise their abilities in ways they might not have been able to do otherwise in mainstream venues. For instance, Tony Award–winning director/choreographer Susan Stroman (*The Producers, Contact*) was given an important break at Lincoln Center that would be a milestone in her career.

"I felt that Susan Stroman had the makings of a director and invited her to come here and create a show and direct it. She had never directed before. I thought based on seeing her choreography in a number of musicals she did—some of them great, some of them stinky—that she was always the most talented person involved. Because this is a nonprofit institution, I was able to say, 'Here's some money, go into the basement and direct something.'" Consequently, *Contact,* the breakout "dance musical" hit of the new millennium, was born; it would win several Tonys, including Best Musical and Best Choreography (for Stroman). It opened on March 30, 2000, at the Beaumont, where it ran for 1,010 performances before closing on September 1, 2002.

Costume designer William Ivey Long, who worked on *Contact* and counts Bishop as one of his closest friends, says that what distinguishes the Lincoln Center Theater artistic chief from other producers is his moral rectitude and humanity. "He's integrity plus," maintains Ivey Long. "More and more these days, there are crossroads where you have to decide if you can do that or work there. If you have a moral question, you ask Andre because he takes everything so seriously and really considers things."

Another artist Bishop cites as being given a strong professional boost at Lincoln Center Theater is Bartlett Sher, artistic director of the Seattle-based regional house Intiman Theatre Company. Sher directed the Lincoln Center Theater productions of *The Light in the Piazza* and *Awake and Sing,* and received Tony nominations for direction for both.

Sher, who first met Bishop through the late theater director Garland Wright in the late 1990s, admires Bishop for his shrewd casting eye, impeccable artistic taste, and meticulous organizational skills. He feels these attributes, as well as Bishop's clarity in judgment and guidance, make "what is arguably the finest producing record in New York in the last thirty years," transforming Lincoln Center Theater into a leading nonprofit. Sher, who directed the pre-Broadway tryout production of *The Light in the Piazza* at the Intiman, came along with the show to the Vivian Beaumont after Bishop agreed to import it to Lincoln Center Theater. Having previously worked in regional theaters in the United States and overseas, Sher was impressed by Bishop's approach to producing.

"There is a kindness, there is a deep level of support with Andre," says Sher. "You would say he's hands-on, but at the same time, you feel like you're making what you need to make. He guides every step of the way; he's incredibly skilled and experienced about choices. He's very diligent, so he's on you in terms of making sure things are in place, as am I. He's created this exceptional working environment that is hard to compare to anywhere else. You always feel safe. He does have what I would call a 'velvet hammer' [approach]. If he really doesn't want you to do something, he's very clear about guiding and saying certain things that he thinks you should or shouldn't do. At the same time, you feel so completely supported, and his thinking is so exceptional that he's always been right."

Sher commends Bishop's decision-making skills because they always seem to make sense. "We had a lot of issues about the pit in *The Light in the Piazza*," recalls Sher, "meaning how big the pit was going to be and how it was going to open a certain way. Then we had this idea about putting these grates out to support the pit in a way that we thought would open it up. Actually, it didn't look so good. Andre was absolutely against it. He came charging down and said, 'No, that's not happening. We'll spend whatever money it takes to open up the pit in a proper way.' That's not a good way to do it and that was decided. We didn't have to go back and forth. He just came right in and said, that's what you're doing."

Commercial versus Nonprofit

Bishop also champions the cause of promoting and nurturing young directors. Every year he runs the Lincoln Center Theater's Directors Lab, in which nascent talent (nearly a hundred young directors) get abundant opportunities to stretch and explore their burgeoning potential in a tight schedule for several weeks.

When asked what qualities all good producers should possess, Bishop finds it difficult to articulate because theater is so arbitrary—not to mention the fact that the nonprofit and commercial worlds are so divergent, although he contends that the demarcation separating them is beginning to blur.

"I would be a hopeless commercial producer on Broadway even though we've done plays that have had enormously successful runs and made a great deal of money. I think I don't have to worry about the marketplace the way a commercial producer must. Any commercial theater producer must weigh if this play or musical is something that has commercial appeal. Now in the commercial field, there are producers who are very intelligent, daring, and tasteful; then there are those who put on the biggest piece of crap that anyone has ever seen because they have some insane idea that people want to see it. And often they're right, alas! But the world has so changed. Had I [come onto the scene] a generation previous, I would have been a commercial producer because the Broadway theater was the theater. Plays were affordable—you didn't have to raise that much money; there was a wide variety of stuff. Now, in the nonprofit theater, what you need to have is your own personal and perhaps idiosyncratic taste.

"I have said this many times because I've read it somewhere; I didn't make it up. Producing is simply the intelligent exercising of one's own taste and hoping that others will see whatever you see in the project and then doing it well. You have to believe that something imperfect can become perfect. This buoyant, not foolish, intelligent optimism is vital because if you try to outguess or outthink yourself, you'll find so many reasons not to do something that you'll end up being paralyzed and not doing anything."

One aforementioned trend that disturbs Bishop is how increasingly the line between nonprofit and commercial Broadway theater has become blurred. As Daryl Roth says—which has been repeatedly corroborated by other producers, including Bishop—it's standard practice nowadays to open a new play in a nonprofit theater; then, if it's a hit, it can be moved to Broadway. This way the prospect of losing a bundle of money, though not erased, is minimized.

"I think a lot of nonprofit theaters, for reasons I do understand—and oddly this one is not like that (though I'm sure some people would think we are because we've had some success at producing things ourselves commercially)—have the artistic mission to produce hits. It's a very cynical viewpoint that I have because I've been around longer than people in New York and a lot of theaters produce plays that have commercial options and commercial money in them. When I was beginning at Playwrights Horizons, you would have lost your money if you had done that.

"You can't do a new play first on Broadway—it just makes it safer if you get the reviews in an institution and then move it. You can sweeten the pot, and all of these nonprofit theaters need money. It's hard raising money and keeping ticket prices low. The members here pay $30 to see *The Coast of Utopia*. The box-office prices are much more than that. That's not a lot of money. It's less and less easy to find out what the artistic point of view of the theater is. Often there isn't one except that it be good or entertaining."

Tips for Aspiring Producers

Bishop's advice to budding producers is not astonishing, given his career trajectory: "Go into the nonprofit theater if you're not interested in making money for yourself, because you just won't. It's a different world from when I got into the theater and it's much harder in New York. It's a much tougher town to live in and support yourself in. I worked for nothing at Playwrights Horizons and I supported myself by waiting on tables and doing things because I lived in a very cheap apartment and my expenses were very modest as a single guy. But I was investing in my future—that's harder to do now. I think [aspiring producers] should go into the nonprofit theater, even volunteer if you can afford it. Nose around, work in every area. I couldn't bear to work with one show every three years with ten other producers. I just couldn't do that. I would get bored. So it depends on what your temperament is. If you want to just develop a show or move it from a nonprofit theater and open it, promote it, and hopefully make money, then go into the commercial theater and work for some commercial theater management office.

"But if you really want to be in the theater and what used to be the theater—these institutional theaters *are* the theater. I'm not knocking the commercial theater, but it's just changed. You can't do *The Coast of Utopia* as a Broadway commercial producer—you would be completely insane to! But it's entirely appropriate that we would be doing it."

Ultimately, Bishop would like to be known as a "daring" and "useful" producer, two adjectives he feels would not normally be ascribed to him. "[People might have called me] useful when I was at Playwrights Horizons, but daring, I'm not so sure at both institutions. But I think, in my very modest and relatively mainstream way, that the writers I worked with at Playwrights and a lot of the shows I've done here at Lincoln Center have been very daring. A lot of the directors we've developed at our Directors Lab and in our education program and all that—we're making contributions to the future of the American theater, and I totally believe in that. I think that part of the duty of every institutional theater is to be useful in the larger scheme of giving homes to artists, because opportunities create artists. [We've created that] for artists where they might not have had them. That's what I mean by useful."

Career Highlights

- Prior to becoming artistic director of Playwrights Horizons, was its literary manager, one of the few positions of its kind during the 1970s
- Has worked with renowned playwrights such as Jon Robin Baitz, Christopher Durang, Richard Greenberg, and the late Wendy Wasserstein in nurturing new works
- Succeeded Gregory Mosher as artistic director of Lincoln Center Theater in January 1992
- Developed serious new musicals at Lincoln Center, evidenced by productions of the Jason Robert Brown/Alfred Uhry's *Parade* (1998–1999) and Michael John LaChiusa's *Marie Christine* (1999–2000)
- Began Broadway directing careers of Tony Award winner Susan Stroman and Intiman Theatre artistic director Bartlett Sher
- Started Lincoln Center Theater's Directors Lab, which fosters the talent of young directors

SECTION IV
The Creatives

CHAPTER 8
Margo Lion

"You can't be with her more than twenty minutes without knowing how much she loves the creative process and how much she genuinely admires and protects the people who do it."

—Jack O'Brien, Tony Award–winning director (*Hairspray, Henry IV, The Coast of Utopia*)

Margo Lion

The "Mad Terrier"

Margo Lion may have cut her proverbial teeth stumping for Robert F. Kennedy in his tragically abbreviated 1968 presidential campaign, but little did the Baltimore native know how far and wide she would travel as one of American theater's most astute producers. Not only has Lion, a former teacher, cultivated incandescent talent on the cusp of fame, such as Tony Award– and Pulitzer Prize–winning playwrights Tony Kushner (*Angels in America*) and the late August Wilson (*Seven Guitars*), she has consistently racked up a succession of prestige projects throughout her twenty-five-year producing career, among them the Tony Award–winning *Angels in America* and *Hairspray.* Some, like Kushner's 2004 work *Caroline, or Change*, might not have been commercial hits, but they still lend a cachet to Lion's ongoing and deserved reputation as a top-caliber producer consistently drawn to works of quality.

A Passion Reawakens

Though Lion had always loved to act when she was a young girl, her stage fright put a crimp on any dreams of treading the boards. It was only after she married her now former husband, an aspiring playwright, following six years of teaching in school (and before that, working on Capitol Hill after graduating from D.C.'s George Washington University with a degree in history and politics), that her dormant passion for theater was revived.

"I got into theater because my former husband was an aspiring playwright. He had been accepted to the Iowa Writers' Workshop and we went out there to Iowa for two years ... I really loved playwrights and directors and I always loved going to theater in Baltimore. I used to love to act and I loved the community of directors and writers, so when we came back to New York, I decided I would love to learn how to be a producer."

Because so much of business is done via networking, Lion asked her cousin, the director/choreographer Martha Clarke, if she knew any producers. Clarke suggested Lyn Austin. "[She] had been Roger Stevens's line producer in New York for fifteen years. She had done a lot of Broadway and she decided to go off on her own," recalls Lion. "She started this not-for-profit group, Music-Theatre Group/Lenox Arts Center. It was a little tiny operation—ninety-nine seats.

"[Lyn] was very daring. It was providential; she turned out to be the perfect person for me to work for because she had worked on Broadway for a long time. She had quite sophisticated tastes and wanted to do something that had quite a distinctive personality. Her approach was very artist-mentored and that suited me very well. It was a very fortunate happenstance [to meet her]. So I started working for her—I was in my early thirties at the time. I started by delivering press releases on my bike, with my little boy in

Harvey Fierstein as Edna in the original production of *Hairspray*

the back. I did everything there, from starting off doing that to sweeping dressing room floors—but ultimately trying to raise money, which is what all not-for-profit theaters want. But this was a particular seat-of-your-pants theater."

Lion feels the situation was ideal because Austin gave her a lot of opportunity to develop her own projects, the first of which centered on a gifted playwright named Harry Kondoleon, then still a student at the Yale School of Drama. Lion had seen a piece he had done entitled *The Bride* and wanted to produce it herself at the Lenox Arts Center in Massachusetts, which was under the aegis of the Music-Theatre Group. Lion would produce a few more shows for Austin, including *Metamorphoses* (not the Mary Zimmerman work that won a Tony Award for Best Direction of a Play in 2002) and the Obie Award–winning *Nature,* the latter directed by Clarke. Lion struck out on her own in 1982 with her first project, *How I Got That Story,* about the Vietnam War, done at the off-Broadway house Westside Arts Theatre.

The cost for getting the show off the ground was $150,000, a meager sum by today's standards. But there was a catch, a serious snarl that could have stalled Lion's future career as a producer were it not for her determination and drive.

"I hated raising money!" groans Lion. "I actually raided my own coffers to put some in because I hated asking people for money. I would pick up the phone—I had this office on Broadway—and I would sit there and I would make these calls. And then I would scream when I got off the phone."

Unfortunately, Lion's aversion hasn't eased with time. But she has learned to wax philosophical about it. "Someone once said to me, and this was very helpful, that these people [the prospective backers] are going to give their money to somebody or to a charity anyway. Occasionally you'll have someone nice who's doing it just to make money, but really nobody on any level or with any reputation is going to put money they don't have to lose into a theatrical project. I'm actually very straight with everybody, saying, you can't put money into a show because you think it's going to make money. You put money into a show because you think it'll be fun.

"I started with friends and then I guess one person led to another. I sort of developed this list. But when people lost money, I didn't go back to them. If somebody did make money, then I would go to them the next time!"

Jamming It Up

Around this time, a new and hugely ambitious endeavor was starting to consume Lion. Its development would mark a critical juncture for her, both professionally and personally.

"While I was [at Music-Theatre Group], I was too stupid to know you shouldn't do this, but I decided to originate my own stuff. I thought that would be fun. Actually that was what producers traditionally had done, but that has gone out of fashion right now. I decided I wanted to do a musical about the origins of jazz. I was led to the interviews of Jelly Roll Morton by Alan Lomax when he had been at the Library of Congress at the National Folklore. I became very interested in those interviews. I thought they painted a very fascinating story of a historical moment both in terms of the nation and in the development of the only indigenous art form that is American. So I began this very long process in 1981 of a show that ultimately became *Jelly's Last Jam.*"

Thus would begin a long and arduous trek for Lion. In addition to her self-professed repugnance for soliciting potential backers for money, Lion was an untested commodity in the high-stakes Broadway market. Unsurprisingly, she wasn't being taken seriously—yet.

"I made a bunch of naive mistakes—you know, misjudgments. I asked August Wilson, who had never seen a musical and didn't know how to build these shows, if he wanted to write *Jelly.* I go on instinct—sometimes it's the wrong instinct—but I think the really difficult mountain to climb was financial. The rest you learn, you deal, you adjust. I trust my artistic judgment enough. But I went through really hard times with *Jelly.* I had to put up my apartment, my artwork and stuff, to get money. Luckily, the show recouped."

Another fortuitous event for Lion that transpired around this time was meeting Rocco Landesman, who would become president of the Jujamcyn Theaters, one of the largest theater owners on Broadway. Through Landesman, a Yale School of Drama graduate, Lion became involved with a number of Jujamcyn projects that included Terrence McNally's *Frankie and Johnny in the Clair de Lune* (which she produced off-Broadway for Manhattan Theatre Club in 1987), the 1989 Broadway revival of *The Threepenny Opera* starring Sting, and *The Secret Garden,* which ran on the Great White Way at the St. James Theater from 1991 to 1993. (For the latter two shows, Lion was credited as an associate producer.)

All of these experiences would be the building blocks for a sequence of milestones. The first would be the 1992 original production of *Jelly's Last Jam.* With a book by George C. Wolfe (who was also directing), music by Jelly Roll Morton, lyrics by Luther Henderson, tap choreography by Gregory Hines (who starred as Morton) and Ted L. Levy, and overall choreography by Hope Clarke, the show became a much vaunted critical and commercial hit. And it would become a benchmark that would lead to another, even bigger benchmark in Lion's career: *Angels in America: Millennium Approaches* and *Angels in America: Perestroika,* Tony Kushner's two-part opus on several relationships brought to the brink during the early years of the AIDS crisis as set against the backdrop of Reagan's America. No other play in contemporary American theater would receive as much attention or accolades as Kushner's Tony Award–winning series. (The first installment, *Millennium Approaches,* would also nab a Pulitzer Prize.)

Joan Marcus

Greed is good—sort of—in the Broadway adaptation of the Adam Sandler film *The Wedding Singer*.

Heavenly Achievement

"It was a wonderful opportunity [to produce *Angels in America*]. *Jelly* had opened in the spring of '92 and *Angels* was done in the fall of '92 in Los Angeles [at the Mark Taper Forum]. It had already gotten this rave review from [then *New York Times* theater critic] Frank Rich when it was done in London at the National. Then when it came to Los Angeles, everybody went out to see it. All the theaters, all the producers—everybody. There was this odd kind of contest, this hurdle you had to get over to get the show. One of the hurdles was that Tony wanted to change directors. Who was going to come up with the right director? He had other issues too: Tony wanted the plays (*Millennium Approaches* and *Perestroika*) to be done together, and Rocco had no problem with that."

As for who could direct the epic work, Lion had a lightbulb moment that was just too obvious to her, having just worked on *Jelly's Last Jam.* She suggested George Wolfe. Kushner enthusiastically embraced the idea, but there was a problem: Wolfe was supposed to direct another show. But in the end, it worked out for everyone. "We brought the entire *Jelly* team, the whole physical production, over with George—this was his first show on Broadway—to work with Tony," recounts Lion. "And then, because of my familiarity with him along with [fellow producer and creative director of Jujamcyn Theaters] Jack Viertel, I line-produced the show, and that was a thrill." (For more on the development of *Angels in America,* see the chapter on Jack Viertel starting on page 41.)

According to the Producers Guild of America Web site (*www.producersguild.org*), a line producer "performs the producer functions involved in supervising the physical aspects of the making of a motion picture or television production where the creative decision-making process is reserved to others, except to such extent as the line producer is permitted to participate." Other film sites define a line producer as someone who oversees the budget of a film or a star's salary. But Lion has a different definition for the type of line producing she does.

"It's always hard to make a distinction in this business because then you'll get people who'll say, 'Oh, I know Suzie Q, and she's a producer,' when really all Suzie Q has done is raise money. I said [I line-produced] because there were a hundred different people above the title with *Angels in America* who were wonderful to put money in it, but in terms of day-to-day operations of the show, it was really Jack and myself. That was thrilling because it's a fantastic play and it gave me an opportunity to be at the beginning of that relationship between George and Tony, which was a wonderfully dynamic collaboration. I could pinch myself. Two of those shows, *Jelly* and *Angels,* sort of established the position I now have. Then I went on to do other things, like August Wilson's *Seven Guitars, Elaine Stritch at Liberty* [winner of the 2002 Tony Award for Best Special Theatrical Event], and then *Hairspray.*"

Begetting Hairspray

Lion got involved with developing what would become the musical adaptation of the kitschy John Waters 1988 film after watching a VHS copy of the film while bedridden with a cold. The irony was that when she first saw the movie when it was released in the late 1980s, she didn't like it; but after seeing it again while sick, the producer in her saw in it viable source material for a musical (and no, the Baltimore setting had nothing to do with it!).

"I believed it had all the elements that were up to a certain standard of a musical: It had larger-than-life central characters, there's something they want, something they have to overcome, and a resolution. But the thing I really look for is a specific personality to the material, a point of view, a voice. John Waters is something of an idiosyncratic voice. But I never thought of it being the kind of hit that it's been. I wanted to do a show about young people and I wanted there to be a lot of dance because we were all coming out of the 1980s and early 1990s, when there really wasn't a lot of dance. Dancing came back with *Crazy for You,* but still we had all these English musicals. Then I wanted to do something celebratory—I liked the fact that there were significant scenes in the show, but I just did it because I thought it would be fun to do."

Inspired, the proactive Lion optioned the rights to *Hairspray* and then went to work getting a writer. She approached composer Marc Shaiman in the late 1990s, who brought Scott Wittman to the project, and together they penned the lyrics and music; Lion also chose Mark O'Donnell to write the book (which he did with Thomas Meehan). Director/choreographer Rob Marshall had initially signed on to be the director until another project, the soon to be award-feted film version of Kander/Ebb's *Chicago,* beckoned. Marshall was out, replaced by Jack O'Brien, veteran director and longstanding artistic director of the eminent Old Globe Theatre in San Diego.

Hairspray first opened out of town at Seattle's 5th Avenue Theatre in early 2002 before opening on Broadway at the Neil Simon Theatre on August 15 of that year. The show became a mammoth success, snaring nine Tonys. Besides Best Musical, awards went to Best Original Score, Best Actor in a Musical (Harvey Fierstein), Best Actress in a Musical (Marissa Jaret Winokur), Best Featured Actor in a Musical (Dick Latessa), Best Costume Design (William Ivey Long), and Best Direction of a Musical.

Hairspray was a project that strongly appealed to Lion because it was about an outsider, as was *Jelly's Last Jam* and *The Triumph of Love.* This theme of characters precariously poised on the margins of society, always wanting to gain entrée but never quite succeeding, strikes a visceral chord with Lion, as do subjects that may not necessarily be commercial.

When Commerce Doesn't Merge with Art

A prime example of a work that was significant for Lion but, unfortunately, did not recoup its investment, was the 2004 production of *Caroline, or Change.* The work, which debuted at the fabled off-Broadway venue the Joseph Papp Public Theater, featured a libretto and book by Tony Kushner and music by Jeanine Tesori. Dealing with the tenuous relationship between a maid and the motherless son (a Kushner alter ego) of the household by which she is employed, the piece, which takes place right before the 1963 assassination of President John F. Kennedy, garnered raves when it first opened downtown but lost momentum when it moved uptown to the Main Stem.

A sad tone is heard in Lion's voice when she recalls working on *Caroline, or Change.* It may not have been as lucrative as *Hairspray,* but it did figure into her criteria when choosing a show to produce: "I did *Caroline, or Change* because I thought it was a really important show. You have to honor your relationships, your beliefs certainly, and your vision, and you help the poor dear boys of the theater. You know, musicals are different. I look for something that I'm going to want to work on for a few years to develop it. Also I like to work with young or new artists who are new to the Broadway stage."

Could *Caroline* have been "saved" had it played indefinitely at a smaller, off-Broadway venue? Lion utters an emphatic "no."

"It had to have been done on Broadway. It was important—that was our feeling. We felt that Tony Kushner, in terms of what he had brought with *Angels in America* and for the particular themes in *Caroline, or Change*, such as the poetry, was extraordinary. We thought it belonged on Broadway because Broadway, whether we liked it or not, is the final point."

It's this type of tenacity and strong convictions that have earned Lion profound admiration and respect in the theater community. Jack O'Brien feels these are the very qualities that make Lion a superb and uncommon producer, in addition to being a wonderful friend.

"She's very clearly at the very top of my list [of producers]. I think she's a woman of integrity and sensitivity," he says. "She's a real person and not a mechanic. And she's not a power broker. She's someone who cares about the art form and, more importantly, about the people who are doing it. You sense that immediately, you sense her humanity. That's rare in this business, it really is. Very often producers want to be titular creators—not midwives—not people who, as the expression goes, 'have your back.' Margo does, and as a result, because she's so honest with what she knows and what she doesn't know, she doesn't hedge her bets—she doesn't lie to you, so you know where you stand with her. You wouldn't think that would be a paramount thing for producers to have in their back pocket. But many of them don't. Many of them have their own insecurities, and they're compensating because they want to be you or they want to control you, which is not the same thing. I never feel that Margo wants to control me. I think she wants to edit me, and I need editing."

Another thing that makes Lion highly unusual for a producer, according to O'Brien, is that she can admit when she makes a mistake. For instance, after Lion had approached O'Brien to direct *Hairspray* (after Marshall dropped out), O'Brien was insistent that his friend and colleague, the Broadway choreographer Jerry Mitchell (*The Full Monty*), also be brought on to the project. Lion had her doubts about Mitchell's suitability for the project but, in the end, O'Brien's judgment prevailed—but a lot of that had to do with Lion's flexibility and willingness to listen.

"The great thing about Margo is that she's just such intrinsically a collaborative woman," says O'Brien. " I call her the 'mad terrier' because she gets an idea in her head and she goes with it. As she did when she didn't think Jerry Mitchell was the right choreographer for *Hairspray*. But if you speak sensibly to her, she listens to you. She doesn't shut you out—she doesn't have preconceived ideas—and as a result, like a creative person, her ideas swing back and forth. You can work with her because she's not rigid in that respect. Once you give her your opinion and once she's convinced of it, she will kill for it."

Adam Epstein, a young Broadway producer who was only twenty-five years old when Lion asked him to be her partner for *Hairspray,* concurs with O'Brien's assessment. Throughout his association with Lion, the early part of which he considered to be that of a "mentor/mentee relationship," he always hailed Lion for being fair-minded and willing to hear both sides of an issue when troubleshooting. But at the same time, she's not a doormat either.

"She's incredibly humane but incredibly tough-minded," says Epstein, whose most recent collaboration with Lion was as one of many backers for *The Wedding Singer.* "It's her humanity that helps leaven what can otherwise be some very hard decisions we have to make. This is very important because people treat people so badly as a rule, but at the same time, we're on the firing line, having to make some tough decisions. And anytime there's any bad news for anybody who's emotional and creative, we come off as villains. The truth is, anyone who's in our shoes would have to do the same things to sustain huge payrolls and try to remain profitable. But she brings that [humanity] to the table. She's wonderful with the creative team. And I think she genuinely cares about the art and about what her name is on what she does."

Always a Teacher

When Lion isn't producing, she can be found these days at New York University teaching graduate musical theater students about producing and how to take charge of their career. Imparting knowledge to young people is important to the former teacher from Baltimore, as is knowing what makes a good producer. "Patience, persistence, and passion," she reflects. "And I should add to that, a point of view. The point of view really has to be flexible. For example, when I thought about doing a show about Jelly Roll Morton, it wasn't at all the show George ended up with. You have to be flexible enough to respond to and receive all the input from the people you hire to create the material."

Any advice for aspiring producers?

"Don't do something you aren't really passionate about. Only produce those things that you believe in and would want to see yourself, because you never know what the outcome could be. There are all kinds of different producers. But this happens to work for me because it allows me to be creative without really doing anything. And I'm a people person and I feel very, very fortunate."

With so many distinguished credits attached to her name, one long-running show (*Hairspray*) currently on the boards, and doubtless others in the wings, Lion is a force to be reckoned with and much more.

Career Highlights

- Worked on Robert F. Kennedy's ill-fated presidential campaign
- Started working as an assistant to producer Lyn Austin
- Developed and produced *Jelly's Last Jam,* which opened April 26, 1992 on Broadway and closed September 5, 1993
- Was one of two lead producers for the *Angels in America* two-part series performed on Broadway
- Developed and produced *Hairspray,* which opened August 15, 2002 on Broadway

CHAPTER 9
Daryl Roth

"She's a very strong lady but she couches it in a very soft, velvety way. It's kind of fun when you see there's steel underneath,"

—Charles Busch, playwright (*The Tale of the Allergist's Wife*)

Daryl Roth

The Nurturer

It was the most difficult decision she ever had to make as a producer—and the one that would test her wherewithal. But the choice Daryl Roth made then, as painful as it was, only heightened the already massive respect she had built among her circle of fellow producers: It was closing the 2005 pre-Broadway production of *Mambo Kings*, the musical adaptation of the 1992 film. Though she was already a hugely successful producer both on and off-Broadway and had

Carol Rosegg

Kathleen Turner and Bill Irwin in the Broadway revival of *Who's Afraid of Virginia Woolf?*

been a force to reckon with for over a dozen years, Roth had never encountered a dilemma as insurmountable as what she faced in San Francisco, where *Mambo Kings* played prior to its expected move to New York City's Broadway Theater.

"We did a workshop that looked fabulous," she recalls. "It was feeling like it was all fitting and working well with the creative team. Then we went to San Francisco for our out-of-town tryout and it just did not work. It was a huge disappointment. I opted to abort it. I was working with my son Jordan (who is now at Jujamcyn) on it. We had worked on it for nearly two years. It had just felt like we were doing everything we could, but it was going off the tracks and it just wasn't good enough to bring to New York. It was a very hard decision. The train has left the station and you're saying, 'Wait, I don't think I can open this in New York because I don't think it'll be successful.' That was the hardest, most challenging, and most disappointing for me . . . [but] time was running out. We had a theater booked, which we couldn't take the time to hang on to any longer in order to take the time necessary to fix it.

"It was a huge decision to make and no one wants to make that decision because, well . . . for many reasons: You have a family of people you're work-ing with and you're saying, 'Okay, we're going to Broadway and this is our out-of-town show.' Then you have to go and say, 'Well, I don't think it's in our best collective interest to continue.' It's a horrible thing—it's like having an abortion, in a way."

Onward and Upward

Roth came to her vocation midlife after raising a family in New Jersey and working as an interior decorator. As she states repeatedly, she is a natural-born nurturer; being a mother, every project in which she invests her time and energy, she tends to as if it's a child.

Although she's moved on to subsequent projects, such as the 2005 Tony Award–winning revival of *Who's Afraid of Virginia Woolf?*, the painful memory of the *Mambo Kings* debacle still sticks in her craw. To Roth, it is emblematic of the disappointment she normally feels when a show she pro-duces does not work—yet magnified tenfold.

"I get postpartum depression after every play that closes or doesn't work. I get very sad. I feel very responsible for everyone involved—too much so. I guess [it comes through] in the way I produce with my need to nurture, to be involved with everybody, and to make everyone a happy family. I think each production is like a family, and the well-being of how happy they are or how dysfunctional they are means a lot to me. And so I'm distraught."

Does she ever tell herself that she can learn from failure when something doesn't work? "I say that too, but I also say to myself, I wish this didn't affect me so much. I think producing is an emotional commitment to a piece of work and many people. You feel that responsibility toward them as if they're members of your family. You don't want to let them down when something doesn't work."

Actress Debra Monk, who first met Roth back in 1991 while working on the doomed Broadway musical *Nick & Nora*, praises her mix of poise, warmth, and generosity. "[When I first met her] I thought she was everything I wanted to be: beautiful, smart, successful—a real creative mind and such a family-oriented person."

It's an association that she prizes on both a personal and professional level: One year, Monk, who is one of the stars of *Curtains*, received the Daryl Roth Creative Spirit Award, a cash award of $10,000, which Roth has been "quietly" giving out annually to gifted theater artists the last few years; and unlike other producers she has worked with, Monk considers Roth to be a friend. "I think she's one of our great producers. We're lucky to have her."

Unintentional Hit-Maker and Award Magnet

If *Mambo Kings* represents the nadir of Roth's near twenty-year producing career on Broadway and off, there has been a spate of hits, many of which would earn Pulitzers and Tonys, such as *Wit, Proof, The Tale of the Allergist's Wife*, and Edward Albee's *Three Tall Women* and *The Goat*, that have more than compensated. In addition to her busy producing schedule, Roth has owned two downtown off-Broadway theaters (both of which bear her name) for ten years: the Daryl Roth Theatre, formerly the Union Square Savings Bank, which was the seven-year home for the zany Argentinean daredevil aerialist/dancers De La Guarda; and DR2, once an annex to the bank, now a ninety-nine-seat space tailored for new plays and smaller casts.

Inside Roth's luxurious Manhattan office, the walls are bedecked with dozens of Tony Award nomination citations she has received over the years; several Tony Awards sit on her cramped desk. Photos of her, flanked by relatives, friends, and luminaries like Edward Albee, adorn the top of a mahogany credenza facing the wide window that affords visitors a glorious panoramic view of New York City. The accoutrements are material evidence that Roth is at the pinnacle of her profession, and yet prior to 1988, her only tangible connection with theater was as a lifelong audience member who adored it. This interest would segue to a new—and unexpected—career.

"In 1988, I was asked to be on the board of City Center, which at the time was developing a musical theater program that ultimately became Encores. While I was not experienced, people on the board [such as then chairman Howard Squadron] knew of me and my interest in theater. I was on the musical theater committee with Richard Maltby, who was hired to be the chair; he was a knowledgeable person in this area."

The First Show

Maltby, a seasoned director and lyricist (*Song and Dance*, *Baby*), had been collaborating with friend and writing partner David Shire on some songs that were to be performed at a Manhattan cabaret. Having befriended Roth through City Center, Maltby invited her to see the show, though at that point, it was just "individual songs held together by the thread of relation-ships." Roth saw it and loved it.

"The songs to me were breathtaking. They got into my heart immediately because most of the songs dealt with changes in your life, doors closing, other doors opening, being open and willing to see what the next step in life will be. It was a wonderful night.

"At the end I said to Richard and David Shire, whom I had just met through Richard, 'This should be a show. If this talks to me, then it's got to talk to other people in my age group or younger or older.' Each song was a story . . . and had a personal message. One song was about taking care of aging parents; another was about new relationships, everything in life you can think of. They said a young man who works in general management came in and was interested too. 'So why don't we put you two together and see if anything comes of it?' I said, 'Great!'"

Roth met with the man, Michael Gill, who currently works in Las Vegas producing musicals; both decided to produce the Maltby/Shire songs as a revue that would later be known as *Closer than Ever*. They wanted to mount it in the summer of 1988. Maltby, who had worked at the famous Williamstown Theatre Festival in Williamstown, Massachusetts, introduced Roth and Gill to key people there. A programming slot was available for one of their smaller venues and that is where *Closer than Ever* got started. It was very well received.

After the Williamstown run, Roth and Gill looked for an off-Broadway theater to move *Closer than Ever* and found it with the Cherry Lane Theatre; it would play there for nine months. Though the show was not a broad com-mercial hit and reviews were decidedly mixed, Roth trusted her instincts and kept the show going because she loved it and thought it would be a word-of-mouth show.

"I was involved in every aspect of the show, learning as I went, because believe me, I didn't know what I was doing. They didn't have the Commercial Theater Institute then," she laughs. "I had no preparation other than a pas-sion, a love, and a tenacity to make this really work. Not only was that the first production I ever did, but it was the first time I had to understand what the decisions are that a producer has to be prepared to make—both hard and easy, both smart and not so smart—all led by your instinct, yet you have to be aware of what the facts are.

"For example, when the numbers weren't really growing, I would go every night and see people being touched and happy and sad—going through this whole range of emotional response. I said, 'Well, people are going to walk out of here and tell people to come—I'm sure of it!' Meanwhile the general manager is saying to close this show and take your losses because the [box-office sales were not increasing]. I think because I was new, because I loved it so much and I truly believed people would come, we kept it going. And it turned out to be the right decision."

Since the off-Broadway run of *Closer than Ever*, a plethora of theater companies across the country have staged the show, according to Roth. Also, she says many actors like to use the Maltby/Shire songs from the show when auditioning because they're both easy to sing and they all tell stories that run the emotional gamut.

Working on *Closer than Ever* served to be an excellent tutorial on producing. For almost a year, Roth learned about advertising and marketing, albeit on a smaller scale. It also gave her a crash course on fundraising, a necessary occupational evil all producers must grapple with. The cost of producing *Closer than Ever*, a four-person show with understudies during the 1988–89 season, was $350,000. With no track record, Roth turned to family and friends to raise that sum.

"I would say that those people who helped me get started did it because they wanted to support me. It wasn't so much about the project, because who do you go to when you first start out? People you know, people whom you hope will support your effort and believe in what you believe in."

The Art of Fundraising

Now with oodles of experience, awards, and recognition under her belt, Roth has a cadre of investors she likes to refer to when taking on a project. But as everyone in life has a certain aesthetic, so do her donors. She always bears that in mind when approaching specific individuals on certain projects. To show good faith to prospective backers, she invariably invests some of her money in projects to demonstrate her unshakable belief in them. She also strives to maintain good relations with investors, always keeping them abreast of production developments, even sending out press releases. But she never tells them a show will be a "slam dunk" either. The economics of theater producing are way too risky to make such an outrageous statement. And Roth's investors are too wise to fall for such cheap sales patter. Like some of our other producers, Roth loathes soliciting others for money. But she takes it in stride.

"[You have to ask yourself], what are you as a producer, or what am I as a producer, here to do? After *Closer than Ever*, it became very clear to me that

I wanted to do things, mostly drama—although I am doing some musicals—about subjects that were challenging that perhaps other producers weren't looking at because they might not have seemed very commercial at the onset, but that's where I felt I could find a niche for myself.' Cause here I am, I'm the new kid on the block, not such a young chick at that point, and I wanted to do something where I could make a difference in a small way. So what I looked for, or rather, what I was drawn to, were smaller plays that had the ability to push emotional and intellectual buttons.

"In the early 1990s, off-Broadway was great—it was really flourishing. You could do plays for $400,000 off-Broadway and be okay and people would come. I know now the pendulum has totally swung back to Broadway in terms of good plays that are challenging. But in the early 1990s, nobody was taking those chances at all. Luckily, I didn't have to support my family this way, so I had the luxury of being able to choose work that spoke to me and that I really wanted to get behind and put out there for other people to experience. I didn't have to look first and say, 'Okay, is this going to make a lot of money?' Even today, when I see people who are starting in this business—young, middle-aged, or whatever—I say, 'Here's the really important thing: Don't do anything you don't love and don't do it for the wrong reasons, because it may surprise you.'"

To Wit

Roth found that out very quickly when she produced Margaret Edson's Pulitzer Prize–winning *Wit*, at New York's off-Broadway, tiny ninety-nine-seat MCC Theater during the 1998–99 season. The play, about a brilliant English professor who's terminally ill with ovarian cancer, seemed like an obvious hard sell, but Roth didn't care. She fell in love with the play and took it on, even though she never thought in a million years it would recoup its investment. She was wrong. The show turned out to be an unqualified financial and critical smash.

Roth got involved with *Wit* when it was done out of town at Long Wharf Theatre in New Haven, Connecticut. She had come to know Kathleen Chalfant, the star, and the artistic director Doug Hughes; she had also been sent the script. "I read it and thought it was magnificent," Roth recalls, "but I wasn't able to make a decision on it based on reading what was written on the page. So [the play's agency] said, 'Well it's going to have a production up at Long Wharf.' So I said, 'Great!' I went and fell in love with it. But the decision was made to give it one more not-for-profit life to see if, in fact, people would warm to it, because it was a very intense subject. We worked out that it would go to MCC [Manhattan Class Company theater] from the Long Wharf and then we saw that people were responding to this—this was going to be worth taking a gamble."

In January 1999, *Wit* moved to the considerably larger (500-seat), commercial Union Square Theatre, where it opened on October 6, 1998, and closed on April 9, 2000, running for 545 performances. Roth did try to move it to Broadway, specifically the smallest venue on the Old Rialto, the 600-seat Helen Hayes Theatre, but encountered resistance from its owner.

"We felt we had something that would fit beautifully in a smaller Broadway house. It was a decent-size cast, so the economics of it made sense in a small Broadway house. So we went to [theater owner/operator] Marty Markinson after we had these wonderful reviews at MCC and said we would love to produce this at the Helen Hayes. He was nervous about it. To his credit, he was being honest to himself and to his instincts. It turned out not to be the right move, maybe, but quite honestly, we would have done this on Broadway. It would have been bold, but we were very happy to do it off-Broadway. We didn't have another option. It wouldn't have been right in a big house—you needed the intimacy. So the decision was made for us. There wasn't an available house, so the Union Square, which is as big of an off-Broadway house as you'll get, is where we went. I think it lasted longer than it would have ultimately [on Broadway]."

The trek for a straight drama like *Wit* from not-for-profit to commercial is typical, says Roth, because very rarely will a play start off at a commercial venue, whether it's off-Broadway or Broadway. The economics of theater producing, which many times seem akin to investing in shaky stock, block that proposition.

Wit was a shining example where art and commerce successfully intermingled. But what about those other instances where art ends up critically pummeled—what then? For Roth, it's a particular source of vexation, especially when she feels all the creative elements of a production are in terrific cohesion.

"As we know, the critics do have a lot of weight, especially when you're doing Broadway, because people are smart. The best thing for an audience member is to listen to word of mouth from someone they respect. But we know that people read reviews and are very influenced by them, and if the critics unanimously say, go see this, you will probably go see this. If the reviews are mixed, you probably won't go until someone else tells you that you should. However, for the time it takes for word of mouth to travel, with the weekly expenses that have to be met, you may not be able to hold on. [It's very frustrating because] you put on this great product and business doesn't come in."

From September to December 1991, Roth produced *The Baby Dance* by Jane Anderson, which played at the off-Broadway's Lucille Lortel Theatre and dealt with adoption and baby-buying. Though it struck

Mercedes Ruehl, Bill Pullman, and Jeffrey Carlson in Edward Albee's *The Goat* on Broadway, winner of the 2002 Best Play Tony Award.

a deep chord for those who saw it, audiences, for the most part, stayed away because of poor reviews, particularly one written by then *New York Times* theater critic Frank Rich. "To this day, people say they were lucky enough to see it," she ruefully recounts. "God, that was such a good play. It's too bad it didn't have a longer run." The play ran for sixty-one performances.

Driving On

Fortunately, for Roth, her batting average with projects has been exceptional. In fact, for every show of hers that has not worked, there have been a half a dozen that have. Acclaimed shows such as *How I Learned To Drive, Proof, The Tale of the Allergist's Wife, The Goat,* and the recent revival of *Who's Afraid of Virginia Woolf?* have prominently figured in Roth's résumé. What they all bear in common is not just a victorious fusion of commerce and art, but many of these pivotal projects crystallized into being due to relationships with creative talent that Roth has cultivated and maintained.

"I was invited to see David Auburn's *Proof* [at the Manhattan Theatre Club] very early because I had worked with Mary-Louise Parker in *How I Learned To Drive,* and she was starring in *Proof.* She called me and said, 'I think you're going to love this play, Daryl. I'd love you to come and see it.' I went to a very early preview and I adored it. Then I went to the people at MTC and said, 'I'd like to help move this if that's what you decide to do. I'd like to be part of the commercial transfer.'" On October 24, 2000, *Proof* opened at the Walter Kerr Theatre, where it stayed until January 5, 2003, running for 917 performances. It collected a slew of trophies, among them the Pulitzer for David Auburn for Best Drama and Tony Awards for Best Play, Best Direction of a Play (Daniel Sullivan), and Best Actress in a Play (Mary-Louise Parker).

Roth's involvement with *The Tale of the Allergist's Wife* came about as a result of her longstanding association with Manhattan Theatre Club artistic director Lynne Meadow. Knowing that Roth was a big fan of the play's author, Charles Busch, Meadow sent her the script to read. Roth also attended an early preview. Upon seeing it, Roth said she wanted to move it and became part of the producing team when *The Tale of the Allergist's Wife* transferred to Broadway. The show opened on November 2, 2000, at the Ethel Barrymore Theatre, where it played until September 15, 2002, running for 777 performances. Like *Proof,* it also launched a very profitable tour.

Busch, who met Roth when she was one of the producers behind the commercial transfer of *The Tale of the Allergist's Wife,* characterizes his relationship with Roth as a unique one—quite unlike the typical producer/artist dynamic. Like Monk, Busch considers Roth to be a personal friend, as well as a professional champion. What most drew her to him in their initial meetings was her nurturing warmth and personality. Busch also greatly appreciates that Roth knows when to give input and when to stay away to let the artist develop his work.

"I think relationships are very important to her. You just feel that family feeling with her. She is a very maternal person, though she's certainly not old enough to be my mother. That is what feels very different about her [compared to other producers]."

To illustrate his point, Busch relates how during the run of *Allergist's Wife*, he suffered a severe, near-death health crisis. Following surgery, Busch, accompanied by his partner and sister, recuperated at Roth's house in the Hamptons. "She was such a wonderful friend and patron to me," he says, with more than a touch of gratitude in his voice.

Rediscovering Albee

In addition to discovering talent and putting them on the map, Roth prides herself on rediscovering talent, such as when Roth teamed up with producer Elizabeth McCann to produce Edward Albee's *Three Tall Women* at off-Broadway's Promenade Theatre, where it opened April 13, 1994, and ran until August 26, 1995, playing for 582 performances. (The Promenade run was a commercial off-Broadway transfer from the not-for-profit, off-Broadway house the Vineyard Theatre.) Although Albee was a legendary playwright, his work, still actively produced in Europe, had fallen out of fashion with the New York theater community during that period. Not only did *Three Tall Women* resuscitate Albee's dormant career in the States, it further cemented his comeback as one of American theater's most venerable playwrights. For his work on *Three Tall Women*, Albee was awarded the 1994 Pulitzer Prize for Drama.

Since *Three Tall Women*, Roth, along with McCann, has produced all of Albee's plays in New York, which include two much-celebrated hits—*The Goat, or Who is Sylvia?*, a controversial play that explored a taboo topic—bestiality—and was the first play of his done on Broadway in over twenty years; and the acclaimed revival of *Who's Afraid of Virginia Woolf?*, starring Kathleen Turner and Bill Irwin. *The Goat* opened at the John Golden Theatre on March 10, 2002, and played until December 15, 2002, running for 309 performances; the same year, it took home the Tony for Best Play. *Virginia Woolf*, which had special significance for Roth because it was her husband's favorite play (he had seen it on Broadway in the initial 1962–64 run), ran for a limited engagement—from March 20, 2005 to September 4, 2005—but it was highly received and thrived on tour.

The Creative Side

As a producer, Roth feels it's impossible to do everything equally well, which is why she values working with top-notch professionals like Elizabeth McCann, whose background in general management has been a complementary asset to Roth's innate creative gifts. "I learned a lot from working with Liz, starting with *Three Tall Women*. She's an experienced producer and also an experienced general manager, so she taught me a great deal about the business side. I always trust my instincts from the artistic side. I think everybody is either left-brain- or right-brain-oriented; I'm much more on the left brain side—in the creative, I'm much stronger."

Today, unlike the days when megalomaniac impresarios like Flo Ziegfeld or his later counterpart, David Merrick, ruled, independent producers can't help but work on shows in teams that will—hopefully—share a like-minded vision. With so many cooks in the kitchen, is this a recipe for success or disaster?

"It depends on the situation and where you are in the hands-on department. In some cases, you don't have too much to do if you're in a huge group other than participate in the capitalization—that's why you're there. But in most cases, because I'm much more of a hands-on producer, I like to be more involved, certainly if it's something that I'm starting or if I'm in one of the three or four lead-producer seats. The larger these groups get, the harder it is to be involved in the way you might like to be because you need to be very diplomatic. But then you narrow it down to the people who actually are making the decisions. If you're not a general partner, which many times, producers are not—there are one or two general partners—then you want to have a consultation with everything because it's your money." Ultimately, if there is dissension in the ranks about anything, the lead producers or "those at the top of the triangle" will take everyone's opinion into account and make a decision.

Roth maintains that what makes a good producer are several key elements: tenacity, focus, an unbridled love of it, and courage in not being afraid to fail. The latter attribute gives the producer a certain psychological buffer because it allows him or her latitude when picking and choosing a project while deeply considering the fact that not everything will work.

Fostering New Talent

What Roth most relishes about her work as a producer and her legacy to the American theater is how she has been the catalyst for talented artists to fulfill their dreams.

"I feel like I'm an enabler, someone who can help someone realize their dream, whether it's the playwright, the actor or director, any part of the creative team. That's a great position. It also means to me that [I've played a role in the] birth of a project that might not have seen the light of day. I've done a lot of work off-Broadway with plays that might not have run very long; yet a playwright's career started, such as Will Eno with *Thom Pain (based on nothing)* and Jon Marans with *Old Wicked Songs*. I like being in a position of giving people a chance to realize their work." *Old Wicked Songs* ran at the Promenade Theatre from September 1996 to March 1997, while *Thom Pain (based on nothing)* ran throughout most of 2005 at Roth's namesake tiny downtown venue, DR2 Theatre. Both garnered critical raves.

Roth's love of discovering talent and giving them a forum to express it was what led her to become a theater owner. "It's the tenth anniversary that I own this theater [Daryl Roth Theatre]," she says. "This came at a time when off-Broadway was really in need of other places and other venues. Now I would say that's not much the case, but in those days you couldn't find an off-Broadway theater; there were great plays but not enough theaters. I had been walking by that space at the corner of 15th and Union Square East since I went to NYU. It's a beautiful space. I saw a big sign up there one day and I called up the broker. I had wonderful plans drawn to make it into a proper theater. Then I got a call about De La Guarda. Somebody came to me and asked if I would produce and house this strange thing from Argentina that I didn't know anything about. I said, 'Do you have a tape?' They sent me this tape and my son Jordan and I sat in front of this tape for ten minutes. Then we looked at each other and I said, 'Jordan, do you think I'm crazy or could this be fabulous?' He said, 'Mom, this is fabulous. What do you have to lose? The space is open—you haven't built the interior yet and these folks need some high ceilings for flying space.' The rest is history—it came and stayed for seven years.

"While this was thriving, I went and developed a little space behind [the Daryl Roth Theatre] that was part of the bank and made it into a ninety-nine-seat theater [called DR2] where I've produced some work [such as *Thom Pain (based on nothing)*] in the last six years. So the theater downtown is another part of my career. We present things as well as produce. I love having it because it's an opportunity for me to offer it to not-for-profit theaters that don't have their own home. Mostly it's for new writers and new work because it's less risky than doing it in a larger space. It's another part of my career that just enhances what I do."

Roth advises aspiring producers to choose projects for which they have a strong affinity. "It can be anything; it can be quirky, it can be funny, it can be silly, it can be campy, it can be intense. Make sure you love it. Don't think what will other people think, because the first decision is, what do you think? Choose things that really get into your soul and in your heart. Don't be afraid to fail. Be a cheerleader for your work. If you have to wear a sandwich board around the street, then do it."

Career Highlights

- Was on the board of Encores
- First show produced was *Closer than Ever*, which ran at the Cherry Lane Theatre, from October 17, 1989 to July 1, 1990
- Has produced a number of plays, such as *Wit* (1998–2000), *Anna in the Tropics* (2003–2004), and *Proof* (2000–2003), which have won Pulitzer Prizes
- Closed the musical adaptation of *Mambo Kings* before it got to Broadway; this decision won her great respect among her industry peers
- Owns two off-Broadway theaters: the Daryl Roth Theatre and the DR2

CHAPTER 10
Fran Weissler

"She's the momma of the store."

—Walter Bobbie, Tony Award–winning director of *Chicago*

Barry and Fran Weissler at the 1982 Tony Awards, where they picked up a trophy for *Othello,*
their first Broadway project

All That Passion

For twenty-five years, the husband-and-wife producing team of Barry and Fran Weissler has been cranking out a succession of hits interspersed with very few flops. As evidenced by their hugely successful, long-running revival of *Chicago* and its many offspring touring companies, the canny Weisslers have an innate sense of what the audience wants to see. They also have an innate sense for picking projects that often rack up a mass of awards: For their very first outing on the Great White Way—the 1982 production of *Othello* starring James Earl Jones and Christopher Plummer—the Weisslers picked up a Tony Award. But what many in the community do not know was that this so-called inaugural Broadway victory was preceded by nearly two decades of producing and touring the classics on a shoestring budget in the Catholic school system. To say that the Weisslers just stumbled accidentally into success is to ignore the overwhelming evidence to the contrary. With Barry in charge of the business end and Fran overseeing the creative, this personal and professional partnership shows few signs of losing its magical momentum. At the end of the 2006–07 season, they were in the process of bringing back to Broadway the legendary director/choreographer/performer Tommy Tune, who had been on an indefinite hiatus. With the Weisslers at the helm of this vehicle, there's no doubt it will generate the attention, accolades and—most likely—revenue often associated with this highly prolific producing twosome.

Yet theater wasn't always a fait accompli for Fran Weissler. Although the Boston native had minored in drama while majoring in English as a student at New York University, Weissler knew her natural calling was not the stage. "I was reasonably bad," she wryly recalls. "I had a very good voice but I couldn't move." Instead, she got married for fourteen years. Then, after she divorced, she met Barry, whose lifelong dream was to be in the theater. Fran's personal and professional life underwent a 180-degree change.

Poor but In Love

"When we started, he said something about how we have to produce on Broadway," she recounts. "I told him, 'I don't know what you're talking about. We don't know anything. How are we going to produce on Broadway?' I had two children from my previous marriage. I said, I have to be home and I have to be there, where they are until they get to be of a certain age. He said, 'What do you think we should do? I want to be in the theater. I don't want to be in my father's business. I don't want to be an accountant!'

"I said, schools have shows, so maybe we should play schools. So we went to some public schools in our area, which was New Jersey. I remember they said, there's no way you can do a show because we don't charge during school hours and it would be undemocratic. One mother can have five children and some children are wealthy and some children are poor and you can't charge during school hours. You can have something at night. Well, we thought, who's going to want to see the classics at night? Barry wanted to do something with Shakespeare at the time.

"Okay, now we're getting married and we have no money. I had two kids. We were mad for each other except everything else was awful. Except when you're in love, you don't know you're poor. I called my best friend, who happened to be Catholic and I said to her, 'What are we going to do? We can't make a living and I'm going to have to go work at Saks and he's going to have to do God knows what.' She said, 'You're so stupid! Why don't you go to the Catholic schools, because they'll charge during school hours?' I said, 'I never met a nun, I never met a priest, and how are we going to do that, and we're both Jewish!' She [laughed] and said, 'Let me introduce you to my nun, who is Sister Mary at St. Aloysius High School in Jersey City.'"

Fran and Barry met with Sister Mary, who told them that the school was very interested in them producing a play entitled *Everyman*, a Medieval allegory "that's read in every Catholic school in America." Sister Mary told the Weisslers that the school would be grateful to them if they did this because it would help the students want to read the play after seeing it dramatized.

"We thought it was a great idea and said we would do it. We went home and read *Everyman*, which she gave us. Every Friday I called thirty-two schools, and Monday, Tuesday, Wednesday, and Thursday, we made eight appointments at each school. So we had thirty-two appointments and we made them from 9 A.M. to 3 P.M. I came home from 3 to 6:30 P.M to be with my kids and make sure we had an early dinner. Then, 6:30 to 9 P.M., we went to the rectories and the convents. I got to know so many Catholics and so many priests and so many nuns. We booked *Everyman* five days a week. We produced study guides and symposiums after the show, and then the next year we did Chekhov and Shaw."

The Weisslers did make money from their promising theatrical enterprise, but it was far from a fortune. But it didn't matter. They were in love and on their way to becoming full-fledged producers.

"We charged $300 a show. I'm married forty years, so this was forty-one years ago," she says. "We thought that was huge and we got a 20 percent deposit, which was $60 times five days and that was $300. We lived on $300 a week, which was $15,000 a year. We thought we were wealthy. We had nothing. We lived on our deposits. We did this for over eighteen years and ultimately, we had eight companies during that time. And we played across the country. We had a U-Haul that carried the sets and a station wagon that carried the actors."

Paul Kolnik

From the long-running Broadway revival of *Chicago*

Making the Leap to Broadway

After producing shows in the Catholic school system for nearly two decades, the Weisslers soon set their sights on Broadway. How were they able to make the transition?

"We decided it was time to take the plunge," explains Fran. "I remember they were doing Shakespeare at the American Shakespeare Theater in Stratford, Connecticut. Christopher Plummer was doing a show there. James Earl Jones was doing a one-man show on Paul Robeson. We had booked him to do it in our schools. We had never met him but we had booked it through his agent,

Lucy Kroll. Then she called us and said James couldn't do it because Robeson's son felt it was a betrayal of his race; he thought the play *Robeson* was too Uncle Tom. It wasn't strong enough, it wasn't black enough. James thought it wasn't worth alienating people [among them Robeson's son]. So we had to cancel an entire tour, which left us bereft. We were out of our minds. Jimmy's agent said to us, 'We owe you.' Then when we went to see Chris in one of the Henrys or Louies or whatever he was doing at Stratford 100 years ago, we thought, 'Wouldn't he make a great Iago?' Plus, Jimmy owed us, so we put it together."

The Weisslers' first foray into the Great White Way would turn out to be a critical success. *Othello* opened on February 3, 1982, at the Winter Garden Theatre and closed on May 23, 1982, running for 126 performances. The production nabbed a Tony that year for Best Reproduction of a Musical or a Play.

"I remember when we were at the Tonys, we were sitting in the very back," recalls Fran. "Alec McCowen called—and mispronounced—our names when we won. I really believe that was the turning point for us after all of those years of touring the classics in the Catholic school system."

Fran doesn't remember how much that production cost overall, but points out it wasn't much because CBS was one of it primary backers. Which leads to our next question: How does she deal with the onerous task of raising money for productions?

Although Fran repeatedly underscores the fact that Barry oversees the business aspects of their partnership, she is quick to assert that she is also responsible for soliciting donors for money—it doesn't completely fall on her husband's shoulders, yet he is the one who seals the deals.

"We [do have a list of donors we go to]. You know, people have made so much money with us. We have produced twenty-seven Broadway shows and about three of them died; the rest of them didn't, so our people made money. In fact, we look for new people because we don't want all our eggs in one basket, but we don't have a lot of trouble raising money anymore. I always tell new investors always check the résumé of the producer and the director. If the producer and director have both done really well in the past, that's a pretty good sign, but even then you can die."

Like many of our other producers, the Weisslers always put a substantial amount of their own money into each show they produce. It's a sign of their faith in a production that they do so. They also are very honest with investors if they feel a show will not recoup.

"We call and write them letters saying that the show doesn't seem to be doing well and we're concerned," says Fran. [We tell them that] unfortunately you may not recoup your money, but we will try very hard to take care of you in our next show. We do everything we can."

It All Starts with the Producer

Fran feels that as producers, she and Barry not only occupy a very special role in the Broadway firmament, but they make decisions about the creative team that will have lasting ramifications for the show.

"The muscle starts with the producer. The producer is everything in the sense that they decide what the project is going to be and who's going to be directing it. Then you pick the director and soon you have to relinquish that power to the director. And if you trust him, you should. Then the director decides with you who the choreographer is if it's a musical, and the designers, meaning scenic, costumes, and lighting. Then you go to the first rehearsal and the director has to give [the power] over to the actors. And then, starting with the first preview, the audience assumes that power."

The Weisslers' criteria for choosing projects vary. They have staffers in their office who scour the country's theaters looking for projects to develop. Barry and Fran often travel to London to check out what's playing on the West End. But very often, ideas will come to them from anywhere. One time, Fran got an idea to produce *Cat on a Hot Tin Roof* starring then screen siren Kathleen Turner after reading a Liz Smith column in which Turner had been quoted as saying if she ever did Broadway, she wanted to play Maggie in the Tennessee Williams drama. Within minutes of reading this tidbit, Fran found out who Turner's agent was, and met with her at the end of that week. And on March 21, 1990, the Weisslers opened their production of *Cat on a Hot Tin Roof* at the Eugene O'Neill Theater, where it closed on August 1, 1990, running for 149 performances; it starred Turner and, as Fran jokingly points out, "it was all because of Liz Smith."

What is refreshing about the Weisslers is that they never labor under any pretense that they are anything other than commercial producers. When seeking shows to produce, they engage in an ongoing, feverish quest to merge two seemingly irreconcilable entities—art and commerce. With the Weisslers, the word "commercial" is not a dirty word. Years of hard-won experience have taught them it is an economic necessity.

One thing Fran has discovered throughout the years is that when creative collaborations work, they can be magical; when they don't, disaster ensues, and that is when she and Barry need to step in pronto to avert further catastrophe. But it's all worth it in the end.

"You can put together a director with a choreographer and with designers and they hate each other," she says. "You have to always hopefully mediate so those people enjoy each other's company and enjoy each other's creativity and the creative processes. There's nothing more exciting [when it all works]. It's like falling in love. When you hear the music coming out of a piano in rehearsal, when you get into the theater and hear the full orchestra, you almost fall over. It's that exciting. You didn't expect all that. The same is true of the set. You get a sketch and then the designer gives you a little model. Then you walk into the theater and there it is. For us, that creative process is what it's all about. We're very passionate about our work. I love it, I just love it. When I don't hate it, I love it."

Max Vadukul

A sleek and sexy poster advertising *Chicago*

Struggling with a Challenging Show

But as smooth and savvy as the Weisslers are in picking out projects that will garner both critical acclaim and soaring box-office receipts, there was one project they fervently believed in from the onset that caused them a lot of angst: William Finn's *Falsettos,* which had first been produced off-Broadway and was one of the first shows that dealt with AIDS.

"It was Jewish, it was gay, it was AIDS at a time when AIDS was not anything you talked about," recalls Fran. "This was before *Jeffrey* and *Angels in America*. It was Bill Finn's work, which I thought was brilliant and ahead of its time. You laughed and laughed and then all of a sudden, it's a kick in the stomach."

Raising money for *Falsettos,* which opened on April 29, 1992, at the John Golden Theatre and closed on June 27, 1993, running for 486 performances, was an almost impossible chore.

"It was very hard. Nobody wanted it. Nobody wanted to put it in their theater, nobody wanted to put money in it. Barry and I went on the line for that show. We really did. Most of the money was ours—almost all of it. We decided, what's the worst thing? We go bankrupt. But if you're in a creative business, you can start again. It's not terrific and you don't want that to happen. But it isn't like you have a store. So we took that shot and we paid back in twenty-six weeks. That's the one thing I remember about the business end of it. We couldn't believe that it did so well. But it did not do well on the road. You don't do *Falsettos* in Mississippi. It's only when you go around the country that you realize we're not the center of the universe."

Unsurprisingly, Fran's most rewarding project has been the long-running Broadway revival of *Chicago*, which is entering its eleventh year. A commercial and critical smash, *Chicago* has spawned highly profitable tours both in this country and abroad. If *Othello* was a key defining moment in the Weisslers' producing career, then *Chicago* has been their towering achievement.

The Weisslers got involved with *Chicago* after seeing a bare-bones production of it at New York City Center's Encores, which presents unknown, forgotten, or rarely staged classic American musicals with maximum orchestration and minimal staging. The Weisslers saw the show at its final performance and were out of sorts afterward, thinking a line of producers had knocked on composers Kander and Ebb's door, begging to take the show to Broadway. To their shock, they were the only producers who had expressed palpable interest. They were alternately pleased and stunned.

"We couldn't believe it," says Fran. "That's why our names are the only names above the title. We produced it alone. Nobody wanted to give us money. Nobody wanted to give us a theater. Nobody believed in it. I said to

Barry, 'Do you think there's something wrong with us? Nobody wants to do it.' So we called Kander and Ebb back and asked them why no one else was interested in it. They said it's funny because they couldn't figure it out either. They thought it was never going to happen.

"We called some of our friends who are producers and asked them why they didn't want to do it. They said there was no chandelier, no helicopter coming on. We thought, 'Are we lucky?' Because we knew that era was over. And that was all production-driven. *Chicago* was performance-driven. We knew it was time for the story for the actors. That's why the other producers didn't do it. It had one set and one set of costumes. Can you believe how lucky we were?"

The Weisslers' production of *Chicago* opened November 14, 1996, at the Richard Rodgers Theatre. The show nabbed a number of Tony Awards, among them Best Revival of a Musical, Best Direction of a Musical (Walter Bobbie), Best Actor in a Musical (James Naughton), and Best Actress in a Musical (Bebe Neuwirth). An earlier production directed and choreographed by Bob Fosse had opened on Broadway in 1975 and had a two-year run. But it didn't do as well as the Weisslers' production. According to Fran, it wasn't as clean as her show. (Some theater pundits have said the problem with the original show was that it was far too ahead of its time. Judging by the massive success of the still-running revival and the 2002 Oscar-winning film adaptation starring Richard Gere, Renée Zellweger, and Catherine Zeta-Jones, who won an Oscar for her portrayal of Velma Kelly, they may have been correct.)

Walter Bobbie, who first met the Weisslers during that pivotal final Encores performance of *Chicago*, which he also directed, was struck by how passionate and determined the Weisslers were in bringing the show to the Main Stem. One minute he was meeting them at Encores, the next they were having production meetings about the upcoming Broadway revival. For anyone else, it would have been overwhelming, but Bobbie soon adjusted well to the rhythms of the indefatigable pair.

Since that time, Bobbie has forged a strong bond of trust and camaraderie with the Weisslers. He worked with them on the 2005 Broadway revival of *Sweet Charity* starring Christina Applegate and has frequently sought out the Weisslers for feedback and advice on projects they haven't been involved with, and vice versa. Such a reciprocal exchange of personal and professional confidence has rewarded Bobbie with unique insight into the husband-and-wife duo, particularly Fran.

"Fran is a big personality," says Bobbie. "I find her incredibly funny and charming. She is wonderful with the actors and the creative team. I think she and Barry complement each other. I think Barry is incredible—he's a very clever businessman, a very aggressive and ambitious producer with marketing instincts and fearlessness in terms of selling the show. I mean, he will really spend the money and market the show. You can never call Barry Weissler to complain that there are no ads in the paper or that no one knows your show is running. That's one conversation you will never have with Barry." He punctuates this with a laugh.

Brutally Frank Assessments

"Barry and Fran are national treasures," exclaims multiple Tony Award–winning costume designer William Ivey Long, who worked with both on *Chicago*. Based on his past conversations with Fran, Long knows she can be candid—brutally so—when assessing his work, as well as remarkably omniscient about comedy. Once, after Fran went to see a comedic production for which Long had designed the costumes, she called him to discuss his work.

"She said, 'William darling, I saw your show last night. I love your work,'" recounts Long. "Then she proceeded to tell me there was a problem with it. She then talked about comedy, how to produce comedy, and how it is all based on the soul and truth, and how crying and laughing are so close. She went on like this, giving me a breakdown on successful productions of comedic moments. It was a brilliant analysis, except she was talking from experience and she was giving examples. I thought I was genuinely privileged to hear this. I wish I were recording it. It was that good. And that's Fran Weissler."

A typical day for Fran Weissler is one marked by routine yet it's one that she anticipates with relish and energy.

"I start in the morning," she says. "I usually work 9 A.M. to 12 noon at home, and everything I do is phone work. Frankly, I get to the office and I'm on the phone too. But I like to do it in my pajamas, so I talk to my office from 9 to 10 A.M. every morning, and everything they give me, I then do from 10 A.M. to 12 noon. Then I go to the office about 12ish. It depends; sometimes it's quiet if you're not producing. We are very lucky—we seem to be always producing, even now. Although we haven't produced a new show this year (2006–07 season), we have all these companies of *Chicago* that we're opening and touring. We have to keep up the casting in New York. We have to make sure that [*Chicago* director] Walter Bobbie comes every six weeks to see the show. We have to make sure our people are managing it and the dance captains are taking care of it in New York. We have a person who is a director at large who takes care of all the *Chicago* companies because Walter Bobbie obviously can't do that. We're really taking care of our touring company, our Broadway company, our London company, the London touring company, the Denmark company—so we're really doing *Chicago* now as we're preparing to do new shows."

On the future docket for the Weisslers are not only plans to bring Tommy Tune back to Broadway but to do a new musical based on the Amy Heckerling hit 1995 movie *Clueless*, as well as another original tuner involving choreographer Andy Blankenbuehler of *In The Heights*, the sleeper off-Broadway hit musical of the 2006–07 season. Fran is especially pleased that her and Barry's future projects all will be new musicals, with nary a revival in sight.

Trusting Your Gut

Fran believes all good producers should possess "street smarts." They should also learn how to trust their gut instinct as to what shows to produce and what to steer clear of. "Sometimes you want to do something and the person who's involved with it is so difficult and life is so short. We learned that the hard way. When we were young, we tackled everything. But when you get more experience, hopefully you become smarter. You decide that some things are not worth it."

Her advice to aspiring producers mirrors the unceasing ardor Fran and Barry feel about the choices they've made in their careers, the theater in general, and each other.

"It's an incredible commitment and if you're not passionate about it, I mean, really passionate about it, don't do it. Do something else. But if you really want to do it, you have to commit 110 percent and you have to know that you have that thing in your gut about what to produce and what not to. If you don't know that and it's about life itself, then you're not going to know about producing. It's really about what's in your gut and your commitment."

Career Highlights

- Didn't become a producer until she met Barry Weissler, whom she later married
- First show she and Barry produced was *Everyman*, a Medieval allegory for a Catholic school
- Spent nearly 20 years touring plays in the school system
- Hired then unknown actor Robert De Niro in an early production for the schools
- First Broadway production—*Othello* (1982), starring James Earl Jones and Christopher Plummer—ended up being a critical hit; it also led to a Tony for Best Reproduction of a Play
- Produced a 1990 revival of *Cat on a Hot Tin Roof* starring then screen temptress Kathleen Turner after reading an item about her in Liz Smith's column in the *New York Daily News*
- Produced the current long-running revival of *Chicago*, now in its eleventh year; the show opened November 14, 1996 on Broadway

SECTION V
The Entrepreneur

CHAPTER 11
Cameron Mackintosh

*"Mackintosh can be both charming and utterly ruthless, as necessary—
a nice dichotomy for anyone in this business. When he was starting out
and could not afford an office, he had his mother answer their home
phone as "Mackintosh Productions," giving a professional impression.
Talk about making the best of a situation!"*

—John Kenrick, professor of musical theater history at NYU and
Marymount College/ author of Musicals101.com

Cameron Mackintosh

The Supernova

Without a doubt, Cameron Mackintosh was the most financially successful producer (on both sides of the Atlantic) of the late 20th century. Having gotten his start producing shows such as *Side by Side by Sondheim* and *Tomfoolery*, Mackintosh hit the jackpot in 1981 with *Cats*, which, until it was recently supplanted by *Phantom of the Opera* (another Mackintosh-produced show), was the longest-running show in Broadway history. Shrewd, savvy, and occasionally ruthless, Mackintosh is the modern embodiment of a visionary producer who's also an unabashed capitalist: Most of his shows that have made it to these shores have been the linchpin of a huge merchandising effort (T-shirts, cups, etc.) designed to appeal to audiences or prospective ones.

Mackintosh's megamusicals, with their large-scale production values, sprawling casts, and Andrew Lloyd Webber scores, revolutionized American theater, especially the musical genre in the 1980s and 1990s. Surely, anyone who was around in New York City during that period can recall reading or hearing about the much-ballyhooed helicopter used in *Miss Saigon* or the revolving turntable of a set in *Les Misérables* or the unapologetically high-octane melodrama of *Phantom of the Opera*. So successful have these United Kingdom imports been that it's not surprising Mackintosh recently brought back *Les Misérables* for a limited run—even though it had only closed three years before, after a sixteen-year run!

In true indomitable Mackintosh fashion, he attributes the *Les Miz* encore, this time at the Broadhurst Theater, to business and nothing more. "I wanted to bring it back purely because the eighteen-year tour had finished and the production therefore was stopping in America for the first time in many years," he says. "I was offered a perfect theater for it. I had done a smaller reinvented version of it in London. I wanted to do that version in New York; plus we wanted to re-orchestrate the show because the orchestrations are thirty years old. This was a perfect opportunity to just bring it in and do a more playhouse version of the show, which has proven to be far more successful than I thought it would be."

Publicized Dispute

As with so many of our other producers, Mackintosh, who was born in Middlesex, England, on October 17, 1946, is no saint. He has gotten into quite a few disputes with American Actors' Equity, stemming mostly from misunderstandings involving a well-respected British actor he wanted to import to Broadway in a production that started in the West End; he also found the union's chorus contracts to be stupid and archaic.

"The biggest problem I had with American Equity was when they wouldn't allow Jonathan Pryce to come with *Miss Saigon* because they said he wasn't Asian, even though he created the role [of the Engineer in the West End] and was fantastic in it and ended up getting a Tony Award. I said no, it isn't a Eurasian part, and they wouldn't have it. In the end I pulled the show even though it had a $35 million advance."

But it came back when the union realized Mackintosh was not kidding in his resolve to cancel the eagerly awaited show. "It did come back because they backed down," he explains. "What I said to them was, 'Look, the thing about *Miss Saigon* is that it is the most successful musical with a large Asian cast of all time. That's going to create a huge amount of work for the Asian community. Indeed it has; it proved to be a catalyst. They had the right point of view: Asians at that point had not had a lot of exposure on Broadway and in the American theater—really not since *Flower Drum Song* had there been a show that had given them a vehicle. But the way they went about it was wrong and they had to back down.

"I also had a problem with Equity over *Les Misérables* after its tenth anniversary because of the stupidity of American contracts, where you've got a principal contract and you've got a chorus contract, which is an outdated, outmoded form of contract. You can't ever give members of the ensemble notice to quit, so we got into the ridiculous situation where some of the students in *Les Misérables*—because the show was so successful—were in their forties.

Michael LePoer Trench

The cast of *Les Misérables* performs "One Day More"

The directors and I can celebrate that the success of *Les Misérables* was actually giving it the cast that Victor Hugo [author of the novel] would want. Sadly, [American Equity] still hasn't gotten rid of that contract, whereas the British Equity got rid of a two-type tier contract back in the 1970s. It's a curious anomaly that American Equity lives in the dark ages."[1]

Miss Saigon opened on April 11, 1991, and closed January 28, 2001, running for 4,092 performances. Besides Jonathan Pryce, who won for Best Actor, the show also garnered Tonys for Lea Salonga for Best Actress in a Musical and Hinton Battle for Best Featured Actor in a Musical.

Falling in Love with Theater

Mackintosh first became entranced with musical theater at the tender age of seven when he was taken to see *Salad Days*. "It was about a magic piano," he recalls. "It became one of the longest-running British musicals ever. It was like a breath of fresh air after the austerity of the war. It ran about five or six years. I loved it. It had people singing and dancing, and of course, I was captivated. The second time I saw it was on my eighth birthday. I discovered that the person who wrote it was playing piano in the orchestra pit and so, at the end of the show, I marched down the aisle and proceeded to introduce myself. He was very annoyed but he decided to take me backstage and show me how all the scenery worked and the flying saucers that were around the stage, how he miked the piano in the pit. I remember looking around the stage and thinking, 'That's what I'm going to do when I grow up!' That's what I did and I didn't quite grow up."

Later on, Mackintosh enrolled in the two-year stage management course at London's prestigious Central School of Speech and Drama. Unfortunately, his schooling was brief. He was bored stiff and took issue with the head of his program after a year. "I had no interest in Euripides. I wanted to get on with putting on a show," he relates. "Also, the guy who was running the stage management course was always like a sergeant major, shouting at everybody. Saying, you've got to keep discipline—discipline! I always found that sidling up to people and being charming to them got quicker results. So he eventually said to me, 'You've got the smarmy ways of a front-of-house manager. You shouldn't be in this course any longer.' This was 1965. So I went away on holiday, and since I was telling everybody I was going to be a producer since I was nearly eight, I thought I should start doing something about it."

Chucking the training circuit, Mackintosh, following a stint as a "holiday relief" backstage worker in the original West End production of *Camelot*, landed his first professional job as a stage manager for a touring production of *Oliver!* The seminal experience was an eye-opener. "That's where I first got to know about stagecraft and the marvelous scenery Sean Kenney designed, and fell in love with Lionel Bart [who wrote the music, lyrics, and book], and ironically I came to do the show many years later."

Parlaying Determination into a Career

For someone whose name is so closely aligned with musical theater, it's also ironic that Mackintosh's first producing project—at least, the first project where he shared producing credit with partners—was a nonmusical, a drawing room comedy, in fact. "I was working with two other producers. I was doing the advertising and various things around the office—it was exactly forty years ago," he recounts, describing his early career trajectory. "It was a repertory season and the first play was called *The Reluctant Debutante*. And that led to other small tours."

How Mackintosh nabbed this job is a testament to his unflinching persistence and callow unflappability. "I talked my way into it. I met somebody while I was being a stage manager for *110 in the Shade*. They were producing and I got on with them. When the show closed, I went into their office. We were putting on a show in this out-of-town theater and basically, they just shut me up. They put my name on the poster because I was doing as much work as them."

When asked how much that project cost, Mackintosh jokes, "about 100 pounds." But the reality wasn't far from the joke. Mackintosh details what the entire process of raising money for shows was like in those days and how the rigmarole of paying your actors was a never-ending saga of buying more time and hoping the checks wouldn't clear too soon, for fear of its inevitable bouncing outcome.

"I used to regularly put on my tours for 250 pounds a week, and in those days you only could hire the scenery and pay for that in arrears. I used to go, 'I need an Agatha Christie set, I need a fireplace and French windows and some nice pictures and some tea,' and they'd go, 'Send us a check at the end of the week.'

"I paid the actors at the end of the week. One of the spurs to get up early in those days was to go to the 'dole,' as it was called. I used to get there at 8 A.M., when the dole office opened. . . ." Mackintosh would then use the dole money to pay the actors. To fund shows, Mackintosh would borrow piecemeal sums, such as "twenty pounds here and there" from relatives and friends. "I was reasonably pretty in those days. I'd flash my eyelids to anyone who I could squeeze money out of."

But no matter how resourceful or charming young Mackintosh was, problems would still surface, especially when they were related to money. For instance, when he produced his first West End musical—"a terrible production of Cole Porter's *Anything Goes*"—Mackintosh found a backer who, according to him, "turned out to be Walter Mitty. Three nights before I committed the show to opening at an out-of-town theater with extra money put in by me, he confessed to me he didn't have a bean to his name. It was a nightmare."

Salvation was soon found in the form of an affable greengrocer who put "1,000 quid" into the production and kept the creditors at bay. Though the experience might have traumatized someone older and more mature, such incidents were typical for Mackintosh in his early days. Yet it did teach him an important lesson.

"It was literally a hand-to-mouth, day-to-day existence. But I was very young; I didn't think [anyone else producing] theater [had an easier time of it]. If I had been given a lot of money and become a producer, I would have thought, that's it. But because I had never had much money and had begged and borrowed money everywhere, it had seemed that disaster was part and parcel of the theater. Therefore, I just sort of pulled my socks up and lived to fight another day.

"The one piece of advice I was always given was, never welsh on your debts. If you can't pay them, be up front with them. And although I did owe money for the first fifteen years of my producing life, I always paid something to these people and I never lied to them. Once you lose your good name in the theater, it's lost forever, particularly in the British theater, which is so small."

Fraternizing with the Banks

It also helps to cultivate and maintain good relations with banks. "I remember I had a tour after *Anything Goes* of a radio play called *At Home with the Dales*. My friends who were also backers gave me the rights and said, 'This will sort you out after the debacle of *Anything Goes*. We want to help you!' They put the money up for the tour but it proved to be a catastrophe. This long-running radio serial, which had millions of fans in Britain—no one wanted to see it on the stage. It would interfere with their memories that they had while listening to the radio. So three weeks into it, I had to pull this twenty-six-week tour. I had no money to pay the actors. I went to my bank manager, who in those days, prior to any ghastliness of instant communications, had no idea that I owed so much money—the checks hadn't all sort of bounced [yet]. So he looked at me and said, 'What are you going to do about it?' I said, 'I don't know.' He said, 'Well, I'm going to give you, completely unsolicited, 500 pounds if you promise me you will pay the actors. And if you don't pay the actors, Equity will blackball you and you will never be able to resume your career. I have faith that you will survive.' And I did. I closed the tour and went off to work for somebody else for a year and then came back to the business and luckily have been in it ever since.

"But in those days, the way you could gain credit was that you had lots of banks. You had a bank in London, which I did. I had a very good bank in London, and then you had a Scottish bank, which stood in rectitude, and another one in Northern Ireland, and another one in Channel Islands. It took at least three and a half weeks for the checks to go through the system. You managed to buy yourself some time. That's why I look down at the modern system of instant communications with such disdain."

Cats' Rocky Start

What's particularly shocking is the revelation that *Cats,* the show that put Mackintosh on the map in the Broadway theater world, hit a rough patch when it came to attracting interested investors right before it opened at the West End in 1981. Once again, Mackintosh relied on his innate shrewdness and personal charm to get things done.

"I had a few West End successes, but *Cats* proved to be a very hard show for both Andrew [Lloyd Webber, who composed the music to T. S. Eliot's poems from *Old Possum's Book of Practical Cats*] and myself. My deal with Andrew was that we would raise half the money, but he, despite his enormous success at that point, found it hard to raise his money, as I did. But eventually, by hook and by crook, we did. But we didn't actually raise the last 25 percent of the capital until we were already in previews. In fact, the last of the capital was raised on the opening night. When the show later opened at [the Winter Garden on Broadway in 1982], everyone was throwing money at us. The Shuberts put up all the money, and David Geffen. But anyone would have given us money at that point. In London I had to write articles in the newspaper to try and raise money because no one in the business wanted to give us a penny!"

He tried to entice readers/potential donors by telling them that this was a very exciting project—"it was Trevor Nunn [who directed *Cats* and was then director of the Royal Shakespeare Company], and for 750 pounds, you could actually get a piece of this adventurous show. And the people who took us up on it were people who had never invested in theater before."

It was around this time that Mackintosh pioneered the concept of merchandising shows. For him, it was simply capitalizing on the trends of the day and applying them to the theatrical realm.

"To be honest, films like *Star Wars* and *Raiders of the Lost Ark* were doing very well with merchandising, so with *Cats,* which I had had to take over the New London Theatre where the show opened, [I wanted to do the same]. The New London Theatre had a very checkered career because it was a television studio at the time when I wanted it for *Cats*. Andrew and I desperately wanted that space for the show. We had to take over the whole building. So I was running the theater as almost a theater owner as well as a theater producer. And therefore I was able to do whatever we wanted. I thought, well, with this show, why don't we try to do some adventurous graphic, which turned out to be one of the great theater posters of all time.

"It's a natural jumping off. So we decided to put a kiosk there and see how it went, because it's that kind of show that lends itself to tremendous marketing and merchandising. It really took off. And then merchandising for theater suddenly became de rigueur. But it only works with certain shows. Some shows lend themselves hugely to it and the audience wants to take a bit of it away, and other shows, you can't give it away."

Beset with a legion of problems preceding its West End premiere, it's no wonder Mackintosh considers *Cats* to be one of his most challenging projects. "The owners of the New London Theatre so thought the show was going to be a failure that they tried to kick us out before we opened. In fact, they wanted us to sign an agreement that either it came off in three months, or it ran two years. That was a terrible problem because we designed this whole theater to fit the environment, with the brilliant set that John Napier had come up with, and we really couldn't move it to anywhere else." Fortunately, the show, as we know, became a smash and a legend soon to be inscribed in the theater pantheon.

Encountering Surprising Snags

Union problems notwithstanding, another show Mackintosh had problems with was *Miss Saigon*. Its story—an interracial romance between an American soldier and a Vietnamese woman in 1970s Saigon—disturbed potential Broadway investors and theater owners. "I couldn't get anybody interested in it in America, where I originally wanted to produce it. Nobody wanted to do it out of town either. They were all scared to death of the subject matter. And it took me a long time to find a director for it. I mean, at the last minute I got and persuaded Nick Hytner to do it."

Les Misérables, another patented Mackintosh megamusical, was also fraught with obstacles for the same reason that *Cats* had been: Everyone thought its chances for success were minuscule. "With *Les Misérables*, I took the longest gestation period because nobody wanted to get involved with it. It took me two years to get Trevor Nunn to agree to direct it. [Everyone] thought it was going to be a disaster. I mean, with most of the great musicals, everyone else in the business thinks they're going to be the biggest disaster. That's been true since time immemorial. I believe when *Show Boat* opened out of town, even though it was Ziegfeld who was doing it, he wasn't there. He didn't go to the opening; he just heard it had done very well and then he brought it to New York.

"Same story with *Oklahoma!* It opened out of town and they couldn't even sell the opening seats at the St. James."

A Phantom Hit

If Rodgers and Hammerstein were a fabled musical theater partnership, then how did another one—the equally heralded Mackintosh/Webber partnership—begin with *Cats* and continue with *Phantom of the Opera*?

"I really didn't know Andrew very well, but he rang me in January 1980 just to have me out to lunch and get to know me. I was an up-and-coming producer. I had done several revivals—*Godspell*, *My Fair Lady*, and *Oliver!*, and new productions. I did *My Fair Lady* and *Oklahoma!* with help from the arts council. I remember him telling me that anyone who could get the arts council of Great Britain to put up money for those two shows couldn't be a complete idiot. And then they had been quite successful. We had discovered that we had a lot of similar thoughts of where the musical theater was going, what it was like, the dearth of directors, and all those things. At the end of the lunch, we went home and he played some of his settings of the poems of T. S. Eliot. It wasn't anything more than that at the time. Everyone else thought that he was completely mad to want to try and do anything to T. S. Eliot. I thought there was something there. We both thought about doing it as a sort of dance/ballet, maybe a sort of sung song cycle and a double bill with another of his pieces called *Variations*.

"That didn't work. We couldn't get anybody interested in it. But I did feel that if we were going to do something with it, the only two people in England who could stage these poems were Trevor Nunn and [former dancer turned choreographer] Gillian Lynne. I didn't know Trevor very well but I had known Gillian very well because I had done several shows with her."

While Mackintosh was trying to persuade Nunn to come on board to direct *Cats*, a positive development happened. After Webber played ten of his compositions to T. S. Eliot's poems to T. S. Eliot's widow, Esmé, she was so moved that she promptly gave him the rights to them and other unpublished poems, which Nunn later used as a framework to build a scenario for the production. Soon John Napier joined the ranks, and the next year, *Cats* was on the boards.

After the tremendous success of *Cats* and *Les Miz*, *Phantom of the Opera* materialized without a hitch. "With *Cats* and *Les Miz* in the bag, Andrew and I could stand on water," says Mackintosh.

"Andrew had rung me at home in 1984. He said, 'What do [you] think of the idea of doing *Phantom*?' I went, 'Oh, that sounds like rather a good idea.' But he only wanted to produce it with me. He actually didn't want to write the score. He had come across that idea because there was another version that was being done in Stratford East and the director of that version had rung up Sarah Brightman, who was then married to Andrew, to ask her to play Christine. Obviously they had talked about it and it had sparked off Andrew's imagination. So the pair of us went down to see this production and we had rather liked it. We tried to work on it for about a month to see if we could do a better version of it and thought in the end that we couldn't do a better version of it. It was quite good enough as it was. So we decided to do our own version. But we weren't the only people—there were three or four other productions of *Phantom* being staged in other parts of the world. Maury Yeston and Arthur Kopit had one in America and there was another one in the Royal Exchange.

"So we just put it out there that we were going to do one, hoping a few people would drop the idea 'cause they heard we were actually going to do it. But it wasn't until Christmas of 1984 that Andrew said to me, 'Look, I decided that I would like to write the score.' And within four months, we put together the first act. I had already hired [the designer] Maria Björnson the moment I thought about the idea, so we knew that she was going to be the only person I could think of who was going to design a world that would make you believe the story. Andrew, Maria, and I did the first version of it and several months later, after we had done a workshop of it—the first act—Hal [Prince, who directed *Phantom*] came on board."

After opening at the West End (Mackintosh generally works from scratch on shows in London before "recreating" them on Broadway), *Phantom* was imported across the pond to Broadway's Majestic Theater, where it opened on January 26, 1988, and where its longevity remains intact. Among its Tony wins were Best Musical, Best Actor in a Musical (Michael Crawford), Best Featured Actress in a Musical (Judy Kaye), and Best Scenic Design and Best Costume Design (both Björnson).

Passionate Musical-Theater Advocate

What is it about musical theater that makes Mackintosh one of the art form's most fervent champions? "I have to fall in love with the characters and story. Of course, I have to like the score as well. But unless I'm taken by what the show is going to be about, I have no interest in the characters, which doesn't mean I can't thoroughly enjoy a show that is a musical comedy; I can, but I don't actually want to produce a straightforward musical comedy myself very often. I've rarely done it.

"I don't particularly like shows that are about [the upper class]. Most of the subject matter that I've worked on in my life are about ordinary people surviving. That was the key to the great successful run of Rodgers and Hammerstein. All their characters are officiate nuns, girls from the Midwest, cowboys—they're not sophisticated people. They only time they failed was when they wrote about sophisticated people, like *Allegro*."

Mackintosh makes no bones about being a micromanager, but also emphatically qualifies that he is one up to a point, but not completely. Ultimately, it's the play, or in his case, the musical, that should be of paramount importance. "I do care about every single element, from the design of the posters to every note in the orchestration to the playing of the actors and everything. However, my job is to find the very best of people to do those jobs and then to get the best out of them. It's not to do the job for them. The people I've had, in a way, the most tempestuous time with are the result of which have been my best productions. If I didn't have a strong director who would really both question me and question what I'm saying and embrace what is a good idea, I would end up doing their job for them in the wrong way. It isn't healthy for the show, and the shows won't work that well. Occasionally I've hired a weak director who just goes, 'Oh, yes, that's a great idea!'—as opposed to, 'Oh, I'm not sure that's a great idea.' It's a big difference. It's a balancing act."

Dancing to a Fine Partnership

Gillian Lynne, the Tony Award–nominated director/choreographer of *Cats*, who has known Mackintosh for over thirty years, can attest to having weathered some stormy creative differences with Mackintosh in the past—but with wistful affection. Although she had met him earlier, Lynne, a former ballerina, got to know Mackintosh well while working with him on the tour of *The Card*, starring Jim Dale, which later transferred to the West End. She found him a joy to work with and it was reciprocal. Sometimes, however, their mutual affinity could be a thorn in the sides of others.

"He and I were really great buddies in the beginning. He was very bubbly and fun. We shared a light sense of humor. We always used to get the giggles during the director's talks. The director would say, 'Would the producer and Miss Lynne please leave the room?' We had to go outside and get over our giggles. He was very like that. Not to say he wasn't absolutely right on the ball, but he was great fun."

Mackintosh's recipe for success is simple: In addition to being a resourceful entrepreneur and visionary, he is deeply enamored with what he does and with the musical theater genre. Lynne has witnessed Mackintosh's infectious bliss firsthand.

"He has an excellent energy level," she says. "He truly is passionate about the business and about musical theater. He truly loves it. It turns him on. You can love something but it doesn't turn you on. He is actually turned on by it. That really is like a love affair—it really causes a lot of extra energy, which makes him irrepressible. Sometimes that's a bad thing, but it was never a bad thing in my day."

Lynne freely admits to having had heated altercations with Mackintosh, but they always quickly blew over. "We used to have rows, of course, but they were always good rows," she impishly recalls. "He never harbored resentment. We've always been wonderful friends and he used to drive me mad—I've driven him mad often. But the good thing about Cameron is that you can have a great shouting match with him and he doesn't harbor it, as I say. You start the next day as if it never happened."

This was particularly helpful when Lynne started working on *Cats*, an undertaking that required endless—and exhausting—expenditures of attention and time on her part. Thankfully, Mackintosh and Andrew Lloyd Webber, who composed the score, left Lynne to her own devices. The same was true for when Lynne choreographed *Phantom*.

"On neither of those did Cameron ever interfere. Ever. Nor would I have tolerated it with *Cats*, because nobody knew what to do with that and I didn't know what to do [with it at first but I also knew] it was absolutely a choreographer's meat. Then there were these brilliant, brilliant words by T. S. Eliot, and they were beautifully matched by Andrew. So it was a piece of cake, really, because there was so much to build on."

She admits that Mackintosh can be ruthless, though "in his own quiet way," a statement echoed by Richard Eyre, the director of the London and the Broadway incarnations of *Mary Poppins*, when he was interviewed by Philip Weiss in a *New York Times* article dated November 5, 2005: "He can be a bully. But I've never known him gratuitously to bully as it were, as a sort of psychological need. To him what matters more than anything in the world is the project, that is the passion and the thing that he gains his identity from."

When asked if he can be ruthless, Mackintosh is unfailingly honest. "Sometimes you have to be ruthless in that you have to do what's right for the show," he admits. "I never liked being ruthless for the sake of it. But if I have to make a decision—to get rid of somebody or to change a writer because I believe I don't know of any other way to make the show continue—[then I will do it] to give it a chance to succeed. So it's for the greater good. But in the end, the musical theater has always been akin to trench war. And there's something about this art form that gives more pleasure to bigger audiences than anything else in the world, which somehow requires the fire of the trench to create. If I'm the head of that process, I need to be like any good general, someone who's there to make the decisions, takes the fight, and gets it over the line."

In the same *New York Times* interview, held right before the American premiere of *Mary Poppins* and the remounting of *Les Misérables*, Mackintosh was candid about his past successes and recent stream of failures, which include critically lambasted shows such as *Martin Guerre*, *The Witches of Eastwick*, *Putting It Together*, *Moby Dick*, and *The Fix*. "In the end they will be as successful as the public wants them to be," he told the *Times*. "I'm going to be delivering two great pieces of theater. I can't do anything more than that."

Mary Poppins Comes to Broadway

Mackintosh's efforts to produce the musical version of P. L. Travers's Mary Poppins books began in the early 1990s. Travers supposedly loathed the treacly movie; Mackintosh convinced her he would stage a theatrical production that would honor the spirit of her books. Travers was swayed and Mackintosh optioned the rights to Travers's books for $75,000. But Disney, which had at that time started making inroads into legit theater, held the rights to the songs by Richard M. and Robert B. Sherman from the 1964 *Mary Poppins* movie starring Julie Andrews. The media empire looked askance on Mackintosh's involvement. They were afraid that Mackintosh would turn the beloved nanny into "an old and nasty and mean lady," said Thomas Schumacher, current head of Disney Theatricals, to the *New York Times*.

Despite Disney's initial dismissal of Mackintosh's plans, the showman from Middlesex persevered—as always. He commissioned George Stiles and Anthony Drewe to write additional songs for the musical and, in a special presentation before then Disney CEO Michael Eisner and his wife, sang some of the songs himself. Mackintosh's gusto and determination deeply impressed Eisner, later causing him to remark to Schumacher, "You know it's no accident that he's so successful."[2] No surprise that Mackintosh is billed as a cocreator of *Mary Poppins*.

Mackintosh found working with Schumacher to be a highly fruitful experience, especially because both were in sync on a number of things. Hence, there was no power struggle or egos jockeying for attention. "From the time we met, we both knew we wanted the same show," says Mackintosh. "He knew, obviously because I've been at it a lot longer than he has, what I was good at, and I could immediately see what he was good at. We didn't care which one of us did what because we knew it was complementary talents and without Tom, I don't believe *Mary Poppins* would have come together because Tom had completely the trust of Michael Eisner and Disney."

An Early Epiphany

Aside from *Cats*, the other turning point in Mackintosh's brilliant career was a realization years ago: "I learned very early that … the book of a musical is the most vital ingredient. I've always been drawn to the authors of every single one of my shows. Even in my failures, like *Moby Dick*—still Herman Melville is the base of it. Shaw, Updike, Dickens, Hugo—I've always gone to classic stories, and once I discovered that about myself—that the source material for my shows matters to me a lot—that was a good point of discovery. I think it isn't a coincidence that my first West End success, which was a revue, was based on the songs of Stephen Sondheim (*Side by Side by Sondheim*), one of the greatest wordsmiths the world has ever known. I was drawn to the words as well as the music."

Before *Mary Poppins* popped up on the theater landscape, there had been rumors that Mackintosh was going to retire. With the weary note of someone who deplores being misquoted yet again, Mackintosh addresses the industry chitchat with an unequivocal air, as if hoping to set the record straight for once. Not only is he not retiring, but his future plans seem to be rife with many things on the agenda, including an intriguing excursion to the Far East.

"I never said I was retiring," he asserts. "What I've said over the last few years, and it's true, is that I'm not interested in finding the next big new musical. It's partly because my interest in the theater now goes far beyond being a producer in that I own and am rebuilding seven lovely West End theaters. I'm a co-owner of Music Theatre International, which is the biggest secondary rights company in the world. Plus, miraculously, the vast body of shows that I've done over the last thirty-odd years are still going strong.… I've been asked to create the musical theater industry in China. I'm about to go off and do that as well as open seven productions in China. We have a list of about fifteen shows that they want. I mean, I don't choose the shows; I read about the shows that we're going to do but I'm going to help put them on. They're not necessarily all my productions either. But there are only certain shows from the West that they want. They seem to be wanting shows that have really good stories."

Ever the entrepreneur, Mackintosh (as stated above) is one of the West End's leading theater owners. Among the theater he owns are the Prince of Wales, the Gielgud, Queen's, Wyndham's, the Albery, the Strand, and the

Prince Edward. In 1995, he was awarded the Queen's Award for Export Achievement; the following year, he was knighted for his impressive accomplishments in the British theater.

Never for the Buck

Mackintosh's career has been blessed with many ironies, one of which is that, according to him, he has never done a show for purely commercial reasons. In fact, his youthful dream was just to be able to make a living as a producer. Never did he entertain visions of earning a fortune at it.

"It may be the reason why I'm successful, because things never go to plan," he says. "I remember in my early years thinking I'll be able to pay this or that off. I've always balanced the risk of taking many risks but, possibly because I'm a Libran, I've never tipped the scales too far."

Mackintosh feels that all good producers should possess passion and charm, plus "you've got to have an eye. It's one of the dictums that I've found all my life: You put on a play or a musical for yourself and then do it as well as possible and then hope the public will come to it. I think if you try to put on a show that will be a public success, you invariably don't."

His advice to aspiring producers is succinct: "Do what you believe in. That's the thing—nothing else."

Throughout his extraordinary life in the theater, Mackintosh has kept a strangely level head when it comes to his vast accomplishments. Sizing up his legacy, he is paradoxical, very much like the man himself—a combination of surprising modesty and swelling pride slightly seasoned with the bravado and feistiness of his youth.

"I would like to be remembered as the person who raised the standard of musical theater in the latter half of the 20th century to new heights all over the world. What I really know is and what I'm most proud of is the fact that several musicals I have produced will be performed long after I'm forgotten. I firmly believe the future of the theater is always remembered in the writing and the writers. I think I've served them quite well."

Career Highlights

- Enrolled for a year in London's Central School of Speech and Drama in the stage management course
- Landed first professional job in 1965 as a stage manager in the tour of *Oliver!*
- First West End success was *Side by Side by Sondheim*, which opened at London's Mermaid Theatre on May 4, 1976

- Produced the longest-running musical on Broadway, *Phantom of the Opera*, which opened January 26, 1988 at the Majestic Theatre, and is still running after two decades
- Produced *Cats*, which ran from October 7, 1982 to September 10, 2000 at the Winter Garden Theatre and was the longest-running show on Broadway until its record was broken by *Phantom*
- Specialized in creating megamusicals with Andrew Lloyd Webber
- Got into a well-publicized scrape with American Actors' Equity after they initially blocked his request to bring over actor Jonathan Pryce from the other side of the pond to the Broadway production of *Miss Saigon*, which had premiered on the West End (with Pryce originating the role of the Engineer). *Miss Saigon* opened April 11, 1991 on the Great White Way, playing at the Broadway Theatre until it closed on January 28, 2001.
- Pioneered the effort to merchandise shows
- Champions musical-theater writers
- Owns seven theaters in London's West End
- Was knighted by the Queen in 1996 due to his achievements in the British theater
- Currently helping China launch its nascent musical-theater industry

---

Endnotes

1. According to Louise Foisy, business representative for Actors' Equity, "Producers have the option to have principal actors on 'term contract'...and during that block of time, the actor cannot be terminated and cannot leave that show. With principal actors and chorus, producers have the option of using a term contract; principals can be offered one month to one or two years; chorus can be offered six-month riders. The six-month riders for chorus [people] doesn't work the same way; it is an ongoing rolling contract. The producer can control it by offering a six-month rider or not; by the end, it can convert to a standard term contract."

    The termination provision of the term contract also applies to chorus members who sign term contracts. "If you sign one of those term contracts, you can't really be terminated unless you commit egregious behavior," Foisy continues. "[However,] at the end of the block of the time [covered by the term contract], if [the producers] want to, they can replace that person." Still, it can be easier to terminate if the producer has cause; but the actor must get a "written warning" to give him a chance to rectify his behavior. If the producers do not have cause for termination, says Foisy, "then they have to buy that person out." This applies to actors, such as the ones whom Mackintosh sought to replace in his most recent Broadway revival of *Les Misérables*, who work under the term contract.

2. Philip Weiss, the *New York Times*, "To the Barricades Once More," November 5, 2006.

CHAPTER 12
Michael David

"You need to have a great time doing it; otherwise you shouldn't do it, because this is really a stupid thing to do for a living."

—Michael David

Michael David

The Erstwhile Idealist

As one of the founders of Dodger Theatricals, a commercial producing organization that has produced a lot more hits on Broadway than flops (most notably the Tony Award–winning smash musical *Jersey Boys*, about the meteoric rise and fall—and subsequent rise again—of the 1960s singing group the Four Seasons), Michael David may be one of our most successful specimens. But if you close your eyes and listen intently to his voice, inflected with the clipped cadences of his Midwest upbringing, his soulfully earnest speeches on theater interspersed with resigned jeremiads on the necessity of Broadway being a "mutual accomplishment of art and commerce," you'll easily detect the lingering vestiges of the blazing, wide-eyed idealist underneath the now crusty veneer.

Detouring into Theater

A Michigan native, David got his first taste of theater as a teenager: "My uncle was lieutenant governor and he had a friend who ran the stagehands' union, so my summer job started when I was fourteen," he recalls. "It was as a stagehand for everything from the Ford Auditorium in Detroit to a burlesque house. That was an extraordinary experience for two reasons: One, I was backstage in the middle of this magical world of what I would call 'those people'; and two, it paid better than anything. I mean I couldn't believe as an apprentice stagehand how much I was making for the summer!"

Attending Albion College in Albion, Michigan, David did extracurricular theater while pursuing a classical languages major. It was the mid-1960s and David, imbued with the spirit of his generation's altruism, entertained hopes of joining the Peace Corps after college graduation to teach English in Afghanistan. He had been accepted into the program and was eager to do so. But life presented a difficult snag:

"My girlfriend got pregnant, and in those days, you got married if your girlfriend was pregnant. So we got married. I couldn't go to Afghanistan with a twenty-year-old pianist wife who got suddenly pregnant," he relates. "So I applied to [the set design program at] Yale Drama School just because of my parents, really. Getting married was one thing, but if I could go to Yale, then that would soften it. I had a couple of professors who thought I was good when I did extracurricular theater. They recommended me and I got in."

With a new wife and a child on the way, David settled into the New Haven–based Ivy League institution quickly, but not without apprehension. "There were nine of us in the class. It was totally over my head," he candidly admits.

Joan Marcus

(Left to right) J. Robert Spencer, John Lloyd Young, Daniel Reichard, Christian Hoff, Peter Gregus, Michael Longoria, and Erica Piccininni perform "I Still Care" in the Broadway production of *Jersey Boys*. The show was a breakout hit in the 2005–06 season, reaping not only a Tony Award for Best New Musical, but also restoring the fortunes of the then ailing Dodger Theatricals, Ltd.

Seeking a respite, David chose in the middle of his three-year course to take part in an outreach program that took advantage of the then roiling civil rights movement.

"I had joined something called the Harvard-Yale Southern Teaching Program, where they would send wide-eyed liberal white boys and girls to Southern schools to teach. I went to a [small college] in North Carolina to teach for a year. It was a frightening experience for my wife. There were more Ku Klux Klan members at that time in North Carolina than anywhere. We lived on campus, which was both a wonderful thing for us to do but also a terrible thing, because of what was going on outside. So it was a very illuminating experience."

Returning to New Haven a year later, David switched his focus of study to a new interdisciplinary program, theater administration and technical design. This enabled him to combine taking courses on set design and theater administration. During this period, David initiated his first producing venture.

"A friend of mine and I started a not-for-profit company and raised foundation money for it," he recounts enthusiastically. "It was in the ragged section of New Haven, and there we took over a warehouse and basically produced plays, while we were students. Dean Robert Brustein had just come to Yale. He didn't know what he was doing either, so he gave us latitude to mess around."

The Nonprofit Route

David's early producing experience stood him in good stead upon graduation. Harvey Lichtenstein, then head of BAM (Brooklyn Academy of Music), was looking for someone to fill an executive director position at the Chelsea Theater Center, a nonprofit company, which was relocating from Manhattan to BAM. The Drama School recommended David and he soon landed the job.

At this point in David's life, he was in his mid-twenties, with a second child added to his growing family. Standing on the threshold of the 1970s, David embraced his new position with gusto. Working at a nonprofit, in concert with Robert Kalfin, who acted as the Chelsea's artistic director, fed into David's still effervescing bubble of idealism. It was a benchmark period in David's fledgling career because for eleven years, he would preside over some of New York's most cutting-edge and noteworthy productions, some of which would move to Broadway.

"For the first three or four years, people thought we were a black company because we did a lot of plays by various black playwrights. But basically we were upstairs at BAM and a lot of our shows moved. We did *Candide* with Hal Prince, which moved to Broadway and ran for two years. We did the first production of *Yentl*, which eventually became the movie—we moved that. We did *Happy End* with Meryl Streep and Chris Lloyd at the St. James. Early on, the not-for-profit was tiptoeing around whether we could be nonprofit and still do good work and at the same time compromise and do something for the commercial theater. We did a number of projects like that. It was a pretty amazing theater at the time. This was the time when foundations were giving money for the work, not for the bottom line, so we were free for the first five years."

David and Kalfin acquired a club on West 43rd Street and turned it into the Westside Theatre, which would become yet another showcase for provocative works produced by the Chelsea Theater Center. How both men came to purchase the property has an interesting backstory of its own:

"The manager of the club was killed in the street," he says. "The Dursts owned the building and we were put in touch with them by a board member. We turned it over, transformed it into two theaters—an upstairs and a downstairs.

We ran that theater simultaneously with BAM. Out of that experience, I would guess a dozen shows in those ten years moved to Broadway or off-Broadway."

By 1980, David and Kalfin ended their partnership, and as part of the divorce agreement, Kalfin retained the Westside Theatre and the National Endowment money, while David stayed at BAM for another two years at Lichtenstein's request. The staff who stayed with David—Des McAnuff, who had been the dramaturg at Chelsea; Edward Strong, a former student of David's when he taught at Yale ten years after David left; Sherman Warren; and Rocco Landesman, who acted as "cheerleader"—would form the nucleus for a budding theater partnership: Dodger Theatricals.

Two years later, the Dodgers left BAM. Invited by Joe Papp to take up residence at the Public Theater (along with Mabou Mines, an avant-garde theater company based in New York City), David took up the offer.

"We had two seasons there with Joe. In the summer between the two seasons, Sherman and Des did *Henry IV* in the park for Joe. Ed, Rocco, and I moved across the street to the Colonnades Theatre Lab. We were on unemployment, so we needed to do something. We picked up a little show from the Cattleman Restaurant that became *Pump Boys and Dinettes*, which we did over the summer, and decided we weren't going to be begging for money from foundations again. The financial scene changed drastically. The money was tightening up and not going for the work anymore. It was all about the bottom line. We decided we weren't going to beg for money. We were going to do it commercially and that was it. We left Joe and [went on to work as commercial producers]."

Producing by Consensus

Although David has been working with his fellow Dodgers for nearly three decades, ironically he finds producing by committee to be an exhausting, if not contrary, undertaking. The ramifications of it make him cynically wonder about the current state of producing.

"I think democracy and producing have nothing to do with one another. And so I think producing by consensus is a horrible idea," he says with a tone of tired exasperation. "It doesn't work, and regrettably today in our business, it's so insensitive that it's mostly necessary that this large bundle of people gathers together to basically produce things. Some know what they're doing; most don't. It's almost amazing to me that anyone can produce; it doesn't take anything but cash. It doesn't take experience or wisdom or taste. All you have to do is to have enough money to do it. And that's it. People who wouldn't dare fix their toilet without calling their plumber imagine without any other information that they can produce something!

(Left to right) J. Robert Spencer, John Lloyd Young, Daniel Reichard, and Christian Hoff perform "My Eyes Adored You" in *Jersey Boys*

"What I think is most important about my, our, growing up in this business was the fact that at Chelsea for ten years and then the Public for two years after that, we had pretty much the same exact group of people as it turned out: boys from the East who produced probably 150 shows, from wacko British playwrights from the Royal Court to Jean Genet's *The Scream*, which was six hours long, to *Candide*, which was environmental—a wonderful version with Bernstein and Hal Prince.... The Dodgers are the same group of guys for the last twenty-some-odd years who cut their teeth even ten years before that. It's terrific to share responsibility with people you have a shorthand with, practicing this for so long, who share both the victory and more often than not in this business, the defeats together. That's great."

Dealing with Donors

Like our other producers, David never tells potential investors they will recoup or make money from a project—ever. To do otherwise would be unscrupulous, not to mention monumentally stupid, given the high-stakes economics of mounting a Broadway show. But David finds that the Dodgers have assembled a loyal team of donors who believe in what they do, even with the understanding that not everything that goes on the boards will translate into a lucrative smash.

"I think it's because we've done so many of these things—God knows many more have been failures than have been successful—but we're relatively good at it, which doesn't mean we're going to have a hit. It does mean that we've done enough within a certain frequency that we don't forget how we fucked up the first time so that we do remember what we did wrong the next time. I think that is what's good about us and why we may be attractive to investors. We've crashed and burned on a regular basis, but we do have a team of people who are not show-related whom we use frequently, whether it's marketers, ad agencies, press officers, or shops.

"Des is still a Dodger. He left us after *Big River* to run the La Jolla Playhouse. The fact is, we've done a dozen shows with him. [We have a] continuity, which is a rare thing among [producers]. [That] is appealing to a small group of investors. But I must say that it's still very difficult to raise dollars and trade control for the money, which we're not here to do. So yes, there is a loyalty to the people who've been with us for a lot of years, just like there is for creative teams and administrative people, as there is for investors who've been the backbone for our funding."

When choosing a project, David and his colleagues have an interesting mantra: "Do shows you want to see in a manner that doesn't embarrass our children," he says. This doesn't mean, David pointedly adds, that every show is a hit; it means that most of the shows the Dodgers have produced have been projects in which they've unanimously expressed great pride—success notwithstanding.

A Show Becomes a Smash

One show in particular, the aforementioned *Jersey Boys*, the 2006 Tony Award winner for Best New Musical, not only passed this test but also succeeded beyond their wildest expectations. The project came to the Dodger desk courtesy of Marshall Brickman and Rick Elice, who wrote the script for the show. Having produced a number of shows about popular culture and music, the Dodgers were interested. They suggested old friend and Dodger mainstay Des McAnuff as director, saying he was the only one for the job. Brickman and Elice agreed and the project was off and running. But David is quick to note that the idea was really Brickman and Elice's via their script; it was just the Dodgers' smart idea to produce it. After an out-of-town tryout at La Jolla Playhouse, *Jersey Boys* opened on November 6, 2005, at the August Wilson Theatre, where it continues to play to standing-room-only audiences. Recently, a national tour was launched to capitalize on the show's massive Broadway success. David is both gratified and astounded at the extraordinarily auspicious outcome for *Jersey Boys*, especially because the show's opening followed a very dark and bleak period for the Dodgers where they not only had a string of flops, but also lost a major partner.

"I think no one could have imagined it doing as well as it did," he says. "*Jersey Boys* acquired that thing that money can't buy: buzz—and you can't buy buzz. You can set it up, but you can't buy it. Success on Broadway is the mutual accomplishment of art and commerce. It's absolutely mutual. You and I can make shows that we like, and it can close in a flash if you don't do the math right. One can't diminish the need to get the commerce right."

To illustrate his point, David invokes *Tommy*, the highly acclaimed stage musical adaptation of The Who's rock opera, which had been produced on Broadway by the Dodgers in the early 1990s. It had a long run, garnered awards, excited crowds, and yet still closed—sadly—in the red. For the Dodgers, what happened with *Tommy* served as a textbook lesson for what they would not do with *Jersey Boys*, when it was apparent the latter show was on its way to becoming an unstoppable juggernaut.

"In the end, we made *Tommy* too heavy to support itself. It ran, it did wonderfully well, but in the end that math didn't quite work," says David. "Consequently, we placed a good deal more weight on that show than it should have needed, and so it cost too much to run. Also, the tour was too expensive. This thing that was geared for us and right up our alley—the result of ten, fifteen years of work—it was too heavy to run. With *Jersey Boys*, we thought this was a real chance not to make it too heavy. *Jersey Boys* serves our criteria spectacularly well and is one of those rare things that's bigger than a breadbox. There were no plans for its tremendous success; it just busted out."

The tremendous success of *Jersey Boys* was a bit of a karmic payback for David after the Dodgers experienced their nadir in 2004. After suffering a few critical and commercial flops, Dodger Theatricals was hit with yet another blow: Their eight-year Dutch partner, Joop van den Ende of Stage Holding, wanted to sever ties. The resulting loss of capital, coupled with the already mounting debts, precipitated considerable downsizing in the Dodgers' New York City–based office as well as the surrendering of Dodger Stages, a midtown off-Broadway multiplex venue that was built to nurture less-commercial Dodger productions, to its Dutch partner, who renamed it New World Stages. It was a very shaky period for the Dodgers, but one that David found inestimable as a learning experience, particularly in light of what would follow with *Jersey Boys*.

Withstanding the Ups and Downs

"I think any producer who is active in this business knows that life is a roller coaster," reflects David. "We had *Jersey Boys* when we were headed down. I think what was demonstrative about it is the seeming heights that *Jersey Boys* can reach coming from the depths of a couple flops. It's vivid. But if every time you had a flop [or a string of failures], you gave up, it's a waste of a flop because a flop can be unbelievably educational.

"I think [what happened to us in 2004] was just the most public chapter in a very long book of producing. I think people chose that moment to look at us. You have to have a thick skin in this business. Someone says, 'What are you going to do?' The answer is, 'Make the next one a hit!' It's very simple. Our business is very transparent."

Celebrated Broadway costume designer William Ivey Long, who has worked on several Dodger productions, among them the acclaimed 1992–95 revival of *Guys and Dolls*, directed by Jerry Zaks, and *A Christmas Carol*, at Madison Square Garden, lauds David and crew for their formidable organization, unyielding support, and mastery of details. All of these qualities were leveraged to their maximum useage when Long worked on *A Christmas Carol*.

"That ran for ten years," says Long, "and it might come back! That was really huge. That took logistics on [the scale] of an army corps. And they were totally up to it."

Having Fun

David feels his strength as a producer comes from his experience in the business and from an insistence on the importance of enjoying himself in his work.

"Look, we're relatively fun guys," he says jokingly. "People like that. We insist on having fun in this business, which is a really stupid thing to do. And the people we hire to work with us are those we have fun with. Sometimes we crash and burn; sometimes we don't. The fact is, we do believe that time is more important than money, so we try and plan for everything. I think we've grown up to be very responsible parents for shows, and that includes after they open. The real key when you open a show on Broadway is to guarantee that you can run long and that you can take the most accurate temperature as to whether the thing you love will be loved by anyone else and support itself."

Which leads to the scourge of many a producer's existence—critics. What does the formerly idealistic, now pragmatic, David think about these potentially poison-penned aisle sitters and their make-or-break influence on his shows?

"Critics are necessary indicators that exist, but the fact that critics come early and all at once cannot be the only indicator of a show's success," he says. "So it's really important that you have enough money so you [can tweak a show before it opens] and not confuse timeliness with accuracy."

Yet David is brutally honest about how instrumental critics can be to a show's ultimate success. "There's envy there," he continues. "I remember when critics Walter Kerr and Jack Kroll reviewed shows. They didn't feel a need to bludgeon you because they didn't like the thing you made. The fact is that this is really hard to do. Crystallizing [the supposed faults of a show] is a vivid demonstration of a lack of understanding."

The Importance of Broadway

If Broadway is such an unwelcome, hostile place for shows, as David states repeatedly, then why continue producing in that terrain? Why perpetuate the torture?

"I think it also has to do with unhealthy urges to win and to win where it's the hardest. But we actually try to make a living doing this, and if you do that, there's only one place to do the wonderful thing we do, and theoretically to pay your staff and give them health insurance.

"For instance, probably the most responsible thing to have done with *Angels in America* was to produce it in a theater downtown and just have it chug away. But *Angels in America* dealt with something bigger than the theater. Yes, you could still be running at the Lucille Lortel downtown, but the fact is that it made the impression it did running on Broadway, being in a place that you could speak loudly, and we all want to speak loudly. ... If a play is a child—a young, fragile, sensitive child—this is clearly the most unwelcoming, most dangerous, most expensive, and most unsupportive place to bring it up. At the same time, it needs this place."

When asked what he feels a producer needs to succeed, the down-to-earth Midwest native bluntly replies: "deep pockets." Doesn't a producer need other qualities to rise to the top of the Broadway rat race? Not necessarily, retorts David. It just depends on what type of producer he or she wants to be.

Upcoming projects on the Dodgers docket include a possible revival of *The Wiz*, and *The Farnsworth Invention*, an Aaron Sorkin (*The West Wing*, *A Few Good Men*) play that opened on Broadway on December 3, 2007, following a tryout at La Jolla Playhouse. A lot of attention is still being scrupulously paid to the Dodgers' golden child, *Jersey Boys*.

"We want to make sure we promulgate *Jersey Boys* properly," says David. "As exciting as it has been, I follow that little cloud wherever I go that says, 'Don't screw this up!' We're taking an awful amount of time trying not to screw it up, to give *Jersey Boys* the longevity it deserves, and we have determined that it's a full-time job.

"Look, it has the potential [to do a lot]. We've never had a show like this and I've done three hundred shows in this city. We want to give it the time it deserves to insure and shape its future. We recognize that it's fruitful and bountiful, and it's our job to make sure it's fertilized properly. It's our responsibility as a responsible parent to basically preserve our child and make more."

Career Highlights

- With others, ran a nonprofit company in New Haven while still a student at Yale Drama School
- First professional job: executive director of nonprofit off-Broadway company Chelsea Theater Center
- Moved many shows from Chelsea Theater Center to Broadway, such as the Hal Prince–directed production of *Candide* (March 10, 1974-January 4, 1976) and *Happy End* (May 7-July 10, 1977), starring Meryl Streep and Christopher Lloyd
- Formerly co-owned Westside Arts Theatre, an off-Broadway theater
- One of several cofounders of Dodger Theatricals
- Prior to going commercial, Dodger Theatricals was a company in residence at the Public Theater while it was under artistic director Joseph Papp
- First show he produced as part of Dodger Theatricals was *Pump Boys and Dinettes*, which opened February 4, 1982 at the Princess Theatre; it closed on June 18, 1983
- Formerly co-owned Dodger Stages (now renamed New World Stages), a multiplex off-Broadway house
- Severed ties in 2004 with Dutch partner Joop van den Ende
- After some artistic and financial setbacks, rebounded big-time with *Jersey Boys*, which opened November 6, 2005 at Broadway's August Wilson Theatre

SECTION VI
The Corporation

CHAPTER 13
Thomas Schumacher

*"If I don't work with him again, my life is going to be very, very poor.
The idea of my not working with him is inconceivable."*

—Bob Crowley, Tony Award–winning designer (*Aida*)

Thomas Schumacher

Priest of Populist Entertainment

Thomas Schumacher lounges on his comfortably chic couch in his charming midtown Manhattan office, decorated with motifs that can only be described as a fusion of nouvelle and vaguely African. With nary an iconic mouse in sight, the nearly fifty-year-old president of Disney Theatrical Productions (or Disney Theatricals) attributes his rise in the Broadway jungle to two things: being in the right place at the right time (in this instance, picking up a backstage phone at the right time); and the boundless generosity he encountered while rising to the top of his field. The latter, Schumacher sharply notes, is one quality that is scarce within the urban parameters he calls the "eight-block radius"—or Broadway—that yawns outside his handsome office. But the infinite magnanimity of others was what sustained him in those early days, when he struggled and scrimped, working several low-paid (or unpaid) jobs simultaneously and living on his credit cards.

Over the years, Schumacher has built a hugely successful career. He has donned a number of hats, most notably as president of Walt Disney Feature Animation, where he oversaw the development and production of twenty-one animated films, including *The Lion King*, *Tarzan*, *Toy Story*, *The Nightmare before Christmas*, *The Hunchback of Notre Dame*, and *Pocahontas*. Now, Schumacher, whose energy is as crackling as is his Hollywood-flavored, deal-making staccato speech, makes a revelation that will be shocking to only the most uninformed outsiders: He's living his dream, his celluloid detour notwithstanding. Ever since he was a boy, he's wanted to be part of a theater company.

A Lucky Break

Unlike some of our other producers who began their careers mid-life, Schumacher always had the theater in his blood. As a youth, he worked in summer stock, community, and school theater. Then, at the tender age of fifteen, Schumacher was hired by the city of San Mateo, California (where he grew up), to run an after-school children's theater program. There he directed two shows over two years while teaching drama classes on the off days. He went on to UCLA, where he majored in theater. Then fate intervened one night for Schumacher, with a phone call that would indelibly change his life.

"I answered a pay phone in a hallway at midnight while striking a show," recalls Schumacher. "A guy I knew was calling the pay phone randomly because it was backstage at UCLA. I was an employee there; I had graduated and this was my last day of employment. The school had given me a job running a professional theater company for three months. I picked up a pay phone and this guy said he needed someone to drive [director/playwright/teacher] Joseph

Chaikin back and forth to the Mark Taper Forum at night for two weeks
to perform *Tongue* and *Savage/Love*, two one-act plays he cowrote with Sam
Shepherd. I said I would do it. I didn't know who Joseph Chaikin was. Four or
five people had said no that night. This guy was working in the casting office
and he was desperate to find someone who would drive Joe and do it for $225
a week. I had a beat-up Volkswagen and no seat belt. I did it and I got to know
Joe; he told [then artistic director] of the Mark Taper Forum Gordon Davidson
that he should give me a job on the night that show closed. Two weeks later, the
Mark Taper Forum called me and gave me a job as a production assistant."

After spending five years at the Taper, where he worked on more than
twenty-five productions, Schumacher continued to cut a swath through the
performing arts field in Los Angeles. He became an associate director of the
1987 Los Angeles Festival of Arts, where he introduced Cirque du Soleil to
American audiences; he also worked at the Los Angeles Ballet, acting as an
assistant general manager.

Then another fortuitous phone call changed his life. "I got a phone call
from Peter Schneider, who was also a theater kid. He had taken this crazy
job at Disney Feature Animation. This was before the rebirth of animation.
He said, 'Do you want to come out here and produce a movie?' I had never
worked in animation. I had never worked in film—I had never produced a
movie. So I went to Disney to be the producer of a movie called *The Rescuers
Down Under* (1990) and just stayed."

Jenn Gambatese and Josh Strickland in *Tarzan*

Schneider first met Schumacher in 1983, when Schneider moved to California to be the associate director of the Olympic Arts Festival for the 1984 Summer Olympics in Los Angeles. Both shared a small office. Schneider later became associate director of the entire festival. Schumacher was hired as a line producer for one of the theater venues. "We've been virtual siblings ever since," says Schumacher of his partnership with Schneider.

The Prodigal Returns

Though Schumacher would achieve great success as one of the chief catalysts behind Disney's animation renaissance, he would eventually find his way back to his first true love—again via an unlikely, roundabout route.

"At some point around the summer of 1994, after *The Lion King* (the movie) opened [for which I was executive producer], I was running development and feature animation while Peter was running the studio. [Then Disney CEO] Michael Eisner asked us to create Disney Theatricals. [The stage musical adaptation of the movie] *Beauty and the Beast* was already on its feet. *Beauty* had come out of the theme parks, and Michael had asked me and Peter to create an ongoing institution to produce theater. Since then we remounted *Beauty*, changed it, moved theaters, and rescaled it. Peter worked on the movie; I didn't, but we inherited it and kind of reshaped it and did tours. Then came the five-year run of *Aida*, which still plays all over the world today, and *Lion King*; we did *The Hunchback of Notre Dame* in Berlin but never brought it to the States, although that will happen. And, of course, *Tarzan, Mary Poppins, The Little Mermaid,* and *King David*."

What prompted Disney to create the theatrical division were two factors. First, the creators of *Beauty and the Beast*, which had its roots in the theme parks, strongly believed and told Eisner that the material would make a great musical. Eisner was swayed, and *Beauty and the Beast* was done with a team comprised of outside theater professionals and those from the theme parks. Throwing caution to the wind, Eisner decided to dip his toes in untested theatrical waters and see what happened. Second, in the mid-1990s, Eisner, a New York City native, was getting involved in revitalizing 42nd Street, once a boulevard of glamour and show-biz glitz that had fallen victim to rampant crime and disrepair over the preceding decades.

After Eisner asked Schumacher to head up Disney's new theatrical division with Peter Schneider, the powerful media titan was given a tour of the erstwhile Ziegfeld gem, the New Amsterdam Theatre on 42nd Street, by then New York City Mayor Rudolph Giuliani. Eisner was scouting for a theater where he could present Disney's family-oriented musicals. Though he was impressed with the still-evident but fading palatial resplendence of the theater, which had been dormant since its Ziegfeld heyday, Eisner was taken aback by the disquieting omnipresence of drug dealers, prostitutes, and porn peddlers plying their trade outside. He wanted theatergoers who were attending Disney on Broadway shows to feel safe and unimpeded by fear. In full magisterial mode, Giuliani reassured the hesitant Eisner that the parade of human dregs would soon vanish. Placing his faith in the indomitable mayor, Eisner was rewarded for it. The owner of the New Amsterdam Theatre, New York State, which had purchased the property in 1992, sold it to Disney for $29 million. From 1995 to 1997, the theater was given a long-overdue renovation. The process of cleaning up 42nd Street had commenced.

In May 1997, Disney Theatrical Productions presented the Alan Mencken/Tim Rice musical *King David* for a very limited run at the newly renovated New Amsterdam Theatre. Soon the street that had once been a harrowing symbol of urban blight had changed into a neon theme park of entertainment geared for excitement-starved tourists and theatergoers anxious to partake of the Disney experience.

Answering Critics

Despite a great deal of opposition to Disney's new presence on Broadway, *Beauty and the Beast* opened on May 18, 1994, at the Palace Theatre, and became a huge commercial hit (though reviews had been less than stellar). It closed during the summer of 2007 to make room at the Lunt-Fontanne Theatre for Disney's next new venture, the stage musical adaptation of *The Little Mermaid*. Thinking about Disney's early detractors thirteen years later still makes Schumacher chafe, especially when it involves a show that's become a revered classic, spawning a virtual cottage industry of tours and productions the world over.

"It's too easy to [dismiss our] detractors because everybody has detractors. But we're identifiable. We're the only producer on Broadway that you can actually identify. Ask someone to name another producer on Broadway!"

Cameron Mackintosh?

"Yes, he has *Phantom* running with Andrew, this brief run of *Les Miz*, and he has *Mary Poppins* with us. Disney and Cameron. Does anybody else's name pop up for you? Because no one else's work feels like a brand. Most people, people who work for us—you will not find a director, a choreographer, or a designer who's worked for us who won't say something lovely because they would do it again in a minute. Alan Eisenberg of Actors' Equity will tell you that actors in Disney shows are treated better—we provide physical therapy and do so much more for them. So people who may have a more negative impression probably have a generally negative impression in life. The theater is a universe of disappointment and failure because 90 percent of what's mounted fails.

Joan Marcus

Another scene from *Tarzan*

"Hundreds of people come in to audition for shows and we cast twenty or thirty. This tells you that at any given moment of time, most people working in theater are not successful. Just look at it from that point of view. Where else do you go where the vast majority of practitioners are unsuccessful at any given moment? It kind of leads you to some inevitable conclusions about having an opinion at what happens in this eight-block radius."

To prove his point, Schumacher poses a rhetorical question: Even without Disney's backing, how long would it have taken him and Cameron Mackintosh to raise the funds for *Mary Poppins*? He believes not long because the idea is commercially salable—the Disney funds and brand notwithstanding. Also, contrary to popular belief, Disney does not have a bottomless well of money that enables it to pour unceasing funds into mediocre shows to insure their longevity.

"It's a false impression that people have. We get financed for the first production. There's no bucket of money we keep going to—the show supports itself," he insists. "If we're going to spend, say, 15 million dollars on *Mary Poppins*, someone else will spend 15 million dollars to mount their new musical. What's the difference? The difference is, I didn't have to make a lot of phone calls to raise the money."

Disney: Like a Nonprofit?

When *Tarzan* opened on May 10, 2006, at the Richard Rodgers Theatre to mostly scathing critical reviews, the show had already received an advance of $14 million, which Schumacher conjectures was probably twice the advance for *Spring Awakening*, the most critically lauded new musical of the 2006–07 season. Again, Schumacher registers exasperation at how Disney is perceived not only by outsiders but also by those in the marketplace. (*Tarzan* closed on July 8, 2007.)

"Disney Theatricals is an institutional theater company. We're not one-off productions, and this is what people don't understand.... We're like a nonprofit. This does not mean nonprofitable; it means we do not bank our profit. Many nonprofits make an enormous amount of money. I have resources that I can apply to a show. *Tarzan* has to make enough money to pay the Nederlanders, from whom we rent the theater, and pay those actors in hand every week. You rise and fall. Every show rises and falls.... You have ten good weeks, ten crappy weeks, and thirty-two kind-of-break-even weeks.

"If you're just producing one musical with an assemblage of people who invested, you don't have any legs under your table. So if your show falters, you falter. But if you set up yourself as an institution and you're producing as an entity—the same thing is true for Jujamcyn—they have a good week here, bad week there—they don't fire all the ushers because that show didn't do well. It's an institution."

Though Schumacher is able to draw upon the Disney reserve when conceiving and staging a show, the idea that the company spends an enormous sum on marketing is a fallacy. "Go add it up," he protests. "I mean, I would say, week by week, *Spring Awakening* outspends Disney by a factor of 100 percent since January 1, 2007. Most people don't know that. You might argue that we spend our money well. Some people will say that when *The Lion King* opened, [there was a constant stream of] full-page ads for the show in the *New York Times*. There were only five full-page ads in fifty-two weeks."

Finding Projects

Schumacher's criteria for choosing and developing a project fluctuate. Clearly, he says, Disney has one of the best catalogs in the business, and that has mostly to do with a common denominator that many people forget: Much of the material Disney has adapted into stage shows—*Mary Poppins, Tarzan, The Little Mermaid, The Lion King,* and *Beauty and the Beast*—was a musical to begin with. "We're expanding something," he explains, "but the vernacular of the piece is already a musical."

Not everything is culled from the Disney catalog. A prominent example of a departure from the norm was *Aida*, the pop musical adaptation of the Verdi opera. With music by Elton John, lyrics by Tim Rice, and book by Linda Woolverton, Robert Falls, and David Henry Hwang, *Aida* opened at the Palace Theatre on Broadway on March 23, 2000, after a less-than-auspicious pre-Broadway tryout. Yet ultimately it turned out to be very lucrative for Disney, even after the Broadway production closed on September 5, 2004, after playing for 1,852 performances.

"It had to fight for its space and had a nice little run by any standard," says Schumacher, summing up *Aida*'s Broadway engagement. "It recouped and made a lot of money. Now a show like *Aida* around the world, this year, next year, with no performances in New York, will make $5 million a year. In foreign productions and high school productions, second-class productions, and amateur productions. So that fuels the ongoing nature of what we've been doing. It's not like the Walt Disney Company that's putting money into [these ventures]—that's where [the profit] comes."

Another example of a profitable show that not only breaks the Disney mold because it did not originate from the catalog, but also never even ran on Broadway, is *High School Musical.* Initially produced as a "charming, light" movie on the Disney Channel, where it "resonated with kids of a certain age," its score was soon released on CDs in record stores, where it became a top seller. Disney Theatrical Productions honed in on the phenomenon and decided to adapt it for theater.

"This year there will be over 1,000 productions of *High School Musical* performed by kids for kids of America. About 5,000 performances. That's a lot. And it's a great thing. We did a stage adaptation. We tested it out with kids. It happened that we let five sort of second-class theaters do productions of it to test the waters. And one of the shows by [director/choreographer] Jeff Calhoun was so good, and there was so much demand for it, that we said, 'You know what? Let's put it on the road! We'll tour it.' [It was all] spontaneous combustion. That can happen."

Some ideas, such as a musical version of the Barry Levinson movie *Tin Man*, or a workshop about the Harlem Globetrotters entitled *Hoops*, do not get past the developmental stage. When Disney expressed interest in adapting A. A. Milne's beloved children's classic *Winnie the Pooh* for the stage, Schumacher met with venerable playwright Edward Albee. Though Albee might be a surprising choice to some, according to Schumacher, he had publicly declared in a number of interviews his affection for *Winnie the Pooh*, calling A. A. Milne one of his favorite authors. Ultimately, it did not get done.

A Crushing Disappointment

Another project that Schumacher devoted a great deal of energy to getting off the ground failed to crystallize because of ill timing and circumstance. He ruefully refers to it as one of his greatest heartbreaks.

"[I was on holiday and] I read a book called *Bee Season*, about a little girl in spelling bees. I sent an e-mail to the States, to the live action studio with Peter Schneider running it. I said, 'You guys should buy the rights because it's a really great idea.' They said, 'Nobody cares about spelling bees.'

"Don't forget that everyone thinks things are obvious after they're successful; no one thinks they're obvious before they've been successful. Trust me. The number of people who told me, Toys come to life in a little boy's bedroom? Who wants to see that? Lions running around singing? Who wants to see that?

"Then I see Jeff Blitz's [2003] documentary *Spellbound*. I loved it. I have lunch with [Broadway producer] Margo Lion. She says, 'I need something now that *Hairspray* is up and going.' I say, 'Margo, everything, every great musical is based on a book, a play, a film, or a social phenomenon. That's just where they come from. And you can also put into the musical category an important social event, such as *1776*. It's based on some preexisting phenomenon or condition or book, play, or film, and most of them are from a book, play, or film.'"

Enthusiastically, Schumacher pitched the idea to his colleague and friend Lion, who promptly dismissed it. Several days later, while on a trip to Italy, Schumacher was having dinner with a group of well-known actors and producers. Again he broached the idea of turning the Blitz documentary into a musical. This time, his enthusiasm didn't fall on deaf ears. His dinner partners embraced the idea and told him he should go for it. Soon thereafter, he called Lion and asked her if he could have his idea back because if she didn't want to do it, then he did. Lion told him she was not interested in the idea. Schumacher then approached Jeffrey Blitz and told him he wanted the stage rights to his documentary. "I wanted to make a musical about these extraordinarily gifted superstar children who are nerds in schools but at spelling bees, they are stars," he recounts.

Schumacher contacted the playwright Doug Wright (*I Am My Own Wife*), asking him if he would be interested in writing the book for the musical based on *Spellbound*. According to Schumacher, Wright had a number of ingenious ideas to "theatricalize" the documentary. Schumacher was especially interested in juxtaposing the stories of the children with those of their parents. Unfortunately, he soon encountered several obstacles that made pursuing the project impossible.

"Jeff Blitz diddled around, didn't take phone calls. A number of people, like Stephen Sondheim, were talking to him about this thing. Meanwhile, it takes me a year of chasing and then he finally goes, 'Well, maybe we should do this.' At that moment, Bill Finn's very charming version, *The 25th Annual Putnam County Spelling Bee*, opens at Barrington Stage and [director] James Lapine gets involved. [It soon moves to Broadway in the spring of 2005, opening at Circle in the Square Theatre.] They turn it into a hit and so now I can't do it!"

The Lion King Roars to the Stage

Spellbound the musical was not to be, in spite of the emotional roller coaster Schumacher rode attempting to bring it to fruition. However, Schumacher has also experienced much anxiety in the preliminary stages of projects that later turned into great successes.

"In the case of *The Lion King*, there was a certain naiveté we all had because none of us had done it before, so we didn't know what not to do," admits Schumacher. "But you can only be innocent like that once. That was challenging because it was almost unproduceable.

"We screened *Lion King* repeatedly inside Disney Studios when we were making the movie. Nobody really liked it very much. The first time we screened it for a real audience at a preview, it was only half animated, with a lot of pencil sketches. The audience went crazy and laughed. Peter

Schneider and I turned to each other and said, 'Who knew it was a comedy?' But it played like a comedy and then it had this big emotional ending and emotional beginning."

Though the film did not garner good reviews, *Lion King* went on to do—to use *Variety* parlance—"boffo" box office. Schumacher feels reviews are not surefire indicators of success. You just have to trust your gut.

Seeking to adapt *The Lion King* into a musical, Schumacher flew to London and met with pop superstar Elton John about composing the music, with Tim Rice writing the lyrics. (The meeting with John transpired after other composers declined the project.) From the inception, he also wanted Julie Taymor to join the team as director/costume designer. Schumacher's trust in Taymor and his uncanny instincts overall paid off handsome dividends, not only in ticket sales but at the Tony Awards, where in 1998 the show won for Best Musical. (Taymor picked up a Tony for her direction and also for her lavish, eye-popping costume designs.) Ten years after the show opened, *The Lion King* remains one of the top tickets on Broadway. But the show's journey to Broadway was rocky.

"The first time we performed the stage show was in Minneapolis in 1997, when it was an out-of-town tryout. The audience went out of its mind but we had no idea how we were going to reproduce it. We kept thinking, we don't know how to get through one more night. Now, all around the world, people are doing *Lion King*—it's a hard show to do; but it has a system, it runs. But when we first did it, it was a mad dash. We literally could not perform the show from start to finish. We had to stop every night in the middle for the first two weeks: We're going to pause and change some scenery. It was pandemonium. Actors didn't know how to make it through."

Yet the show was able to make it work by the time it landed on Broadway; more importantly, it fulfilled audience expectation of what a Disney show should be—larger-than-life, big-scale, colorful costumes and outsize, magnificent sets. Like other Disney shows, says Schumacher, *The Lion King* has that ineffable Disney "magic" that theatergoers are willing to shell out their hard-earned money to see. It's when Disney fails to live up to expectation that they run into trouble.

Schumacher learned this the hard way when he produced a bare-bones musical revue called *On the Record*, which toured the country from November 2004 to July 2005. With songs chosen from the Disney catalog, the show featured production elements that were very simple—the polar opposite to the elaborate production elements that are trademarks for every Disney show on Broadway. Reviews were mixed and ultimately the show did not work, says Schumacher, because it didn't have that "extra gigantic thing" associated with Disney.

Working with Disney

Though some critics may like to take jabs at Disney's fiscal resources, others find those resources to be invaluable. Lighting designer Natasha Katz, who worked with Schumacher on the road tour for *On the Record* as well as the Broadway productions of *Aida* (for which she won a Tony Award), *Beauty and the Beast*, *Tarzan*, and *The Little Mermaid*, enjoys working with Disney for many reasons, one of which is their being able to extend a longer preview and technical rehearsal time, as opposed to other Broadway producers.

"You get a lot of time to go through everything," she says. "You need money to be able to do that ... and give the creative people the tools that they need."

Katz especially enjoys her working association with Schumacher because of what she terms his formidable intellect, infinite energy, and seemingly limitless frame of reference. She also finds him to be an avid champion of the theater artist.

"There's nobody better. We all spend our lives trying to keep up with Tom," she says in a tone that's half joking and half serious. "He's very supportive, and when I say supportive, it's in the sense that he absolutely allows the creative people on the project to do their jobs; he guides us a little bit. He has complete trust in the people who are working for him. But when the time comes for Tom to come in and actually participate, he has very strong opinions on things. There is always room for dialogue and it all sort of gets worked out."

Bob Crowley, the Tony Award–winning designer (*Aida*) who made his directing debut with *Tarzan*, echoes Katz's sentiment about Schumacher but goes one step further.

"I don't think there's anyone quite like him. His knowledge just of the theater and musicals is profound, and he's one of the few people I know who has a huge range of references that actually don't have anything to do with the theater. He's got such a fountain of experience and knowledge. From someone so young, it's kind of amazing. It feels like working with a veteran producer, but it's his youth and enthusiasm and passion that connect with you.

"I couldn't have gotten through [directing and designing the sets and costumes for *Tarzan*] without him. That's the truth. I was doing three jobs at once. It's an enormous kind of burden. I had never directed a musical before; I had hardly directed anything before! The pressure was immense. All the way through, Tom was standing there beside me and just pushing me forward, saying, you really are doing it fabulously. I just had a complete dialogue with him all the way through. I can't think of a single moment when we disagreed, and even if we disagreed or chose to disagree, he would totally respect that it was his opinion or my opinion. He has never ever tried to force his opinions on me, which is what a lot of producers do for a living."

Fulfilling an Obligation

Schumacher feels his mission as a producer is twofold. "Our job is to produce high-quality entertainment—stuff that the audience wants to come and see. Hopefully it enlightens and inspires them. If you do that well and get lucky, you can make money out of it. Just as the goal of any show is to return the investment and pay its investors, my investors happen to be the shareholders of the Walt Disney Company, who are not supervised by the attorney general of New York. My investors are represented by the Securities Exchange Commission (SEC). There's an obligation I have to not be irresponsible with shareholder funds. I have a fiduciary responsibility to give them a good return on their investment—that's why they bought stock.

"People forget that the owners of the Walt Disney Company are not a group of men who wear navy blue suits and sit around a black granite table in Los Angeles. The owners of Walt Disney are children and grandparents and teachers' pension funds. Health-care workers, unions—people own Disney stock, and they bought it because they want to make money. Everyone looks at their stock portfolio or their 401(k) and they forget that they are the exact same people who own the Walt Disney Company."

Schumacher believes that all good producers should possess a strong inherent sense of self. "Everyone is different. I love Margo. We see the world differently and similarly. You have to be willing to do anything you've asked someone else to do. I'm lucky because I grew up in the theater; I've worked a lot. I've been a custodian and I've sold ladies' shoes; I've been a professional dyer and I've been a craftsperson; I've hung lights and I've worked in professional box offices; I've done a bit of carpentry and a lot of different jobs, so I have a lot of knowledge about everything. I'm not uncomfortable in that world. I'm very comfortable onstage; I've also been a performer. So for me, that's a very useful tool. Also useful is that I've been around very big successful things and I've been around and worked with some of the most extraordinary people of our time. For me, all of these have been advantages. Someone else might come into it with a different set of skills."

What advice does Schumacher have to aspiring producers? "Gain experience. Never say no. I've said this at graduation speeches, but look around you because someone in the room may call you [for a job], or you're going to call someone in the room. [Maybe that phone call] is going to connect you to a Tony Award. Have eyes open wider than what's on Broadway. See what people are doing, see theater in foreign countries.

"I can pick up a phone and Edward Albee might not say yes to *Winnie the Pooh*, but he'll have lunch about it. I get to work with [director] Richard Eyre, or Cameron Mackintosh, [Oscar-winning screenwriter] Julian Fellowes, Bob Crowley, Elton John, [director] Francesca Zambello—I can call anyone in the world and say, 'Would you like to try this?'"

Schumacher has no interest in leaving a legacy for the American theater, nor any wish to be remembered. "The reward is in the ability to be part of it."

Career Highlights

- At age of 15, was hired by the city of San Mateo, California, to run an after-school children's theater program
- First professional, post-college theater job was as a production assistant for the Mark Taper Forum
- Met future business partner Peter Schneider when Schneider was associate director of the Olympic Arts Festival for the 1984 Summer Olympics in Los Angeles. Schumacher was hired as a line producer for one of the festival venues
- Introduced American audiences to Cirque du Soleil while working as associate director of the 1987 Los Angeles Festival of Arts
- Worked at the Los Angeles Ballet as an assistant general manager
- Joined the Disney Company in 1988, producing the animated film *The Rescuers Down Under*; became president of Walt Disney Feature Animation (and Theatrical Productions) in 1999, where he oversaw the development and production of twenty-one animated films, including *The Lion King, Tarzan, Toy Story, The Nightmare before Christmas, The Hunchback of Notre Dame*, and *Pocahontas*
- Was asked by then Disney CEO Michael Eisner to start up with Peter Schneider a theatrical division for Disney
- First show that opened under the Disney Theatricals banner was the short-lived *King David*, which ran from May 18 to 23, 1997 at the New Amsterdam Theatre
- Produced the hugely successful, Tony Award–winning *Lion King*, currently in its tenth year on Broadway; the show, which opened on November 13, 1997, is currently playing at the Minskoff Theatre

SECTION VII
The Up and Coming

CHAPTER 14
Roy Gabay

"He's got amazing integrity. He's got incredible intelligence and he loves what he does. He loves this business. There are a lot of people who are just in it for the money. I don't know why they would be—it's not that kind of a business—but there are those people where everything's the bottom line. They don't have a regard for artists the way he does."

—Susan Dietz, coproducer of *The Little Dog Laughed*

Roy Gabay

The Numbers Cruncher

Brooklyn native Roy Gabay is an unassuming, up-and-coming Broadway producer who owes a lot of his success in his relatively short but fruitful career to the fact that he knows how to create a financial forecast and plan a budget. They are the first two elements he considers when he's interested in producing a show, before tackling who the audience might be as well as his potential partners. It's a refreshingly practical and realistic tactic born from another incontrovertible fact about Gabay: In addition to being a prudent young producer, he is also a general manager. Gabay's extensive experience in the latter vocation has laid a solid foundation for the former undertaking.

In the Beginning

Armed with a degree in theater from McCallister College, a small liberal arts college in Minnesota, Gabay set his skills, experience (which included operating the sound for a small Minneapolis theater company), and natural acumen to work in veteran Broadway producer Elizabeth McCann's office. From intern he became a receptionist, then an assistant company manager, then a company manager, and finally, a general manager. It was a career arc that Gabay savored, especially because it led to a very auspicious professional affiliation with McCann, herself a seasoned general manager. As a mentor to Gabay, McCann taught him not only a great deal about general managing but about producing itself.

To Gabay, general managing and producing are almost comparable, except a producer is responsible for raising money whereas a general manager is responsible for all aspects of a production *except for* raising money. Being a general manager complements what Gabay does as a producer.

"I think being a general manager is incredibly important to being a good producer because it allows you to experience every aspect of putting on a show. As a general manager, we're involved in every single area. It certainly informs how the money is being spent and how the work is getting done. I find it invaluable to being a good producer."

Gabay represents a new breed of producers far removed from the old, larger-than-life archetypes whose names were as famous, sometimes even more so, than the stars who acted in their productions. He is normal and down-to-earth—no grandiose publicity stunts or full-page ads bearing his likeness for him. When asked why there exists a dearth of showmen types of producers on the modern Broadway terrain, Gabay chalks it up to how inordinately sophisticated people have become in this cynical age and how easily they can see through such subterfuge.

Tom Everett Scott and Johnny Galecki in *The Little Dog Laughed*

"I don't think that [publicity stunts to drum up attention for a flagging show] is a reliable alternative. The public has gotten too savvy; they're too aware of the various schemes; the Internet has opened up a whole new level of awareness and information. So as brilliant as some of those events were, I don't think we could do the same things anymore and have it be successful."

Segue to Producing

Gabay's approach to producing has been similarly sensible and businesslike, without too much fuss. Because of his general management work, Gabay has forged a network of contacts highly advantageous to his producing career. One of these propitious relationships is with the small, nonprofit off-Broadway Vineyard Theatre. Several years earlier, McCann had seen Edward Albee's *Three Tall Women* (which would win the 1994 Pulitzer Prize for Drama) at the Vineyard and had liked it so much, she decided she wanted to do a commercial transfer of the production to off-Broadway, with Gabay as company manager. During the run, the general manager left and Gabay replaced him. This marked *Three Tall Women* as the first production Gabay worked on as a GM. The play, which ran for two years, fared very well—it toured and also did a stint in London.

"Because of *Three Tall Women*, I had formed a relationship with the Vineyard Theatre, which is where [my first producing project] *How I Learned to Drive* was playing. I was asked to be on the board of directors of the

Vineyard Theatre. When they did *Drive*, it was successful after it opened. [The board] wanted to do a commercial transfer. So they brought some of the money to the table and then they asked other people if they had access to any money. Because of the work I had been doing prior to that as a GM, various investors said to me, 'Look if something comes along that you think we'd be interested in, let us know.' So I stepped up to the plate and raised a substantial amount of money for *How I Learned to Drive* and became an above-the-title producer."

The show moved to the Century Theatre in April 1997 and became a critical and commercial success. Playwright Paula Vogel won a Pulitzer Prize for her work about the incestuous relationship between a young woman and her uncle. The production signified a career crossroads for Gabay.

"It was great for my first show to have been such a hit. It established me as a producer, it established my credibility with investors, and it established my credibility with artists like Paula Vogel and the creative team, like Mark Brokaw, the director."

The production cost $300,000 to mount, of which Gabay raised $50,000. And because Gabay already had prospective donors lined up from his work as a GM, he didn't have to solicit the unsolicited for vast sums of money. Yet raising money is never easy—circumstances notwithstanding.

"I don't think anybody likes [to ask others for money], to be honest. I don't think it's the thing when you get up in the morning you say, 'Gee, I wish I could ask people for money today.' It's a necessary part of our business. I think the only way you can get through it, as least for me, is to be passionate about what you're talking about. I'm not a good salesman—that's not what I do best—but if I have a passion about what I'm trying to produce, I can at least sell it honestly."

How does he deal with calling up backers who may have lost substantial capital with the last production they invested in? Gabay's response reflects his logical, grounded take on the industry and his place in it.

"I think people who invest in this business understand the risk. While no one likes to lose money, they're certainly prepared for that possibility. The way our business works is that the next one could be the one. They're always open to getting a call and they're sophisticated people. They'll make their own decision and decide if that's the project they want. I mean, I've had people that have done lots of shows with me and then I come to them with a bigger show. I'm sure they're going to do it and they say no. And then they're there for the next one. They just say that such and such piece they didn't like."

Taking on the Great White Way

Naturally, it helps when they do like the piece, and if Gabay feels passionate about the work, their infectious enthusiasm can feed off his and become contagious. Gabay's first producing project for Broadway fit this category: the commercial transfer of the Roundabout Theatre Company's revival of Arthur Miller's *A View from the Bridge*, starring Anthony LaPaglia. McCann and Gabay saw and loved the production, which was closing. McCann wanted to produce it on Broadway; this time she asked Gabay to be her partner.

The initial experience of producing on Broadway as opposed to off-Broadway was jarringly different in terms of economics. However, because Gabay and McCann were both producing the show, both could easily pool their resources to get the job done.

"There was a lot more money at stake, so we had to raise a lot more [than you would if it were off-Broadway]. The way we did it is that we raised it jointly because we were working in the same office. We knew a lot of the same people. It wasn't about, 'Well, who are your investors and who are my investors?' It was a joint thing, which was a great thing because it was a shared effort."

A View from the Bridge opened on December 14, 1997, at the Criterion Center Stage Right, and closed at the Neil Simon Theatre on August 30, 1998; it ran for 239 performances. The production snared the 1998 Tony for Best Revival; LaPaglia was also honored with a trophy for Best Actor. Not a bad outing for Gabay's first foray as a Broadway producer.

Yet his most challenging production was one that would arguably be his most acclaimed: Mary Zimmerman's *Metamorphoses*, a stage adaptation of the myths of Ovid, replete with a large swimming pool and a cast full of unknowns. The show, which had opened at off-Broadway's Second Stage shortly after 9/11, had hit a cathartic nerve with New Yorkers with its allegorical tales of love, loss, longing, and redemption. Shell-shocked audiences hungrily welcomed Zimmerman's script with an ardor bordering on therapeutic.

For Gabay, producing *Metamorphoses* would be a pivotal feat in his career, akin to his earlier experience with *How I Learned to Drive*. But with *Metamorphoses*, there were far more hurdles to overcome.

"I was not the first person in line for that show. There were other people who wanted the rights. Ultimately those people couldn't figure out a way to make the numbers work. By the time the show got to me, nobody thought it would be successful, and I was very pleased to prove everyone wrong. I just felt so strongly about that show and I figured out a way, through careful budgeting, etcetera, to make it successful. I was very proud of that experience because a lot of people said they didn't think it could be done. I think that established me also with another group of people."

On March 4, 2002, *Metamorphoses* opened at Circle in the Square, and ran for 400 performances. A few months later, at the annual Tony Awards ceremony, Mary Zimmerman picked up the Tony for Best Direction of a Play.

When Gabay took over the reins as producer of *Metamorphoses*, he thought the production would not recoup on Broadway. Happily, his expectation would be proven incorrect.

"I thought maybe down the line there would be enough productions where we would eventually recoup. When I took the step back to see if it was commercial, I didn't really think it was; but I thought in the trying period following 9/11, it was important to me to do that show." According to Gabay, *Metamorphoses* not only recouped 150 percent on Broadway, but it made even more money through myriad regional productions.

Gabay's feelings about *Metamorphoses* are in line with how he chooses a project: The criteria he uses have nothing to do with a show's bottom-line profit margin.

"I have to connect with it. I can't think of anything I've done just for commercial value—meaning I thought it would make money. I mean, I think the shows I produce are going to make money, but I'm attracted to them because I have a connection to them on some level, emotional, intellectual, whatever it is. Once I have that, I try to look at it and say, 'Okay, can this show that I feel passionate about, can it make money, and can it connect with enough audience to make it possible?'"

Like Betting on the Stock Market?

Being a producer can sometimes be analogous to being a gambler or stock market speculator. Very often you can't help but take chances on something that most likely will not work out. Gabay learned that the hard way with *Frozen*, a critically well-received play by Bryony Lavery, about a child molester/murderer who is confronted by the mother of the child he killed. The show, which opened at Circle in the Square on May 4, 2004, played for 128 performances.

With all the positive buzz surrounding the show in its first flush, Gabay and his team of producers banked on the show winning the Tony that year for Best Play. It lost to *I Am My Own Wife*, a one-man play by Doug Wright about a real-life transvestite German art dealer circa World War II. Gabay and company were crushed.

"I think we all loved the show. It played during a season where it really had the potential to win the Tony Award. We thought if we could win the Tony

Award, it could propel us into a recouping possibility, and ultimately we didn't. I think we were frustrated and surprised. We lost to *I Am My Own Wife*, which I loved as a project, but I'm not sure it falls under the category of Best Play."

Carol Rosegg

Donald Corren and Judy Kaye in *Souvenir*

But Gabay's keen instincts toward *Golda's Balcony*, a one-woman show about the late former prime minister of Israel, Golda Meir, were uncannily on the mark. The show, which opened October 15, 2003, at the Helen Hayes Theatre, ran for 493 performances. It had a built-in audience and more than recouped on Broadway.

Russell Simmons Def Poetry Jam, which played at the Longacre Theatre and ran from November 14, 2002, to May 4, 2003, was another frustrating experience. Apparently, Gabay overestimated Simmons's ability to draw in audiences. (Simmons is a music mogul who cofounded the pioneering hip-hop record label Def Jam; he also has his own fashion label.)

"Russell is a force of nature on his own and he was passionate about that project. I thought that because of who he was, he could do for *Def Poetry*, even though he wasn't in it, what Sean Combs did for *A Raisin in the Sun*. [The 2004 revival, which starred the hip-hop impresario/entrepreneur, was a resounding box-office success and scored Best Actress and Best Featured Actress Tonys, respectively, for Phylicia Rashad and Audra McDonald.] It was so tied to him that I thought that the audience who watches his TV show, buys his clothing, would come out for it, and they did, but in not enough numbers."

Launching *Little Dog*

Gabay's most recent producing project is *The Little Dog Laughed*, a Broadway transfer from the nonprofit off-Broadway Second Stage production that ran during the 2005–06 season. Written by Douglas Beane, *The Little Dog Laughed* is an original satirical comedy about a Hollywood agent and her client, a young, rising movie star who's also secretly gay. Gabay's involvement with the project is emblematic of that old musty cliché: never burn bridges. But a little bit of persuasion leavened with outlasting your rivals also helps.

"I saw the show on the opening night at Second Stage, and at the party, before the reviews came out, I said to the artistic director, Carole Rothman, that I loved the show and, like *Metamorphoses*, I would like to be involved in a commercial transfer to Broadway. The next morning the reviews came out and that was good for everybody. Again, I was not the only one who said that in the course of a couple of days." Ultimately, due to Gabay's past association with Rothman with *Metamorphoses* and with Scott Ellis, the play's director, he was entrusted with the task of presiding over the Broadway transfer.

However, after Rothman handed over the project to Gabay, it was anything but smooth sailing. Firstly, Second Stage wanted the show to move to Broadway in the 2005–06 season, but there was a hitch: There were no theaters available. As a result, *The Little Dog Laughed* had to wait for the start of the 2006–07 season before a theater would be vacant. On November 13, 2006, it opened at the Cort Theatre. Only two performers from the original off-Broadway production—Julie White (as the agent) and Johnny Galecki (as the hustler who falls for the closeted movie star)—remained.

Susan Dietz, a coproducer of *The Little Dog Laughed*—who has enjoyed a long connection with Gabay dating back from the days when her partner, Joan Stein, was the producer for the 1998–99 Broadway play *Side Man* (for which Gabay served as general manager), says he's one of the best producers she's worked with.

"Because of his general management background, he is so aware of his fiduciary responsibilities to his investors and his partners. His management style is realistic but kind. He knows what he's doing. He knows where he has to get to but he's not adversarial. He's very respectful of everyone he works with."

In addition to his considerate treatment of colleagues and talent, Gabay is also shrewd. Nowhere was this more evident than in an incident prior to the start of the 2006–07 Broadway season, when the transfer of *The Little Dog Laughed* was beset by yet another snag.

"[Roy and I] were trying to figure out how we were going to get a theater," recounts Dietz. "We weren't having any luck with the Shuberts [giving us a theater]. Then Roy said to me, 'You know, Julie [White, the star of *The Little Dog Laughed*] is our greatest asset here. She's the one who got all the rave reviews; she's the one who's brilliant in the play.' We knew we were taking her—we just didn't know who else would be in the cast. 'But she's charming,' he said. 'What if we took her up to meet with Gerry Schoenfeld [chairman of the Shubert Organization] to see if she can persuade him?' So Roy called her up and asked her in the most respectful way if she would be willing to go into a producer's office and try and secure a theater. It's kind of an odd thing to ask an actress to do. And of course, Julie is the best sport in the world. She said yes, and Roy escorted her and made it really pleasant for her. She walked into [Gerry's office] and within twenty minutes, we had a theater.... What Roy wanted to show Gerry was that Julie was a star. And he did it! It was such a great idea."

As is the case of many shows that have garnered both critical and commercial accolades, *Little Dog* was not an easy show to produce, according to Dietz. "We had to work for every single thing we got, including Tom Everett Scott [who played the closeted movie star] and the theater and the money. It was not one of those slam-dunk things. Every once in a while, you get a slam dunk where it's obvious and you raise the money quickly and your cast and creative team come together very fast. But sometimes you really have to work at it and you have to believe in it. I think that perseverance is probably one of the greatest assets a producer can have. You can look at that in a couple of ways. You can say it's perseverance, but you can also say it's stubbornness, bullheadedness—I'm going to do this no matter what. Sometimes you say, I shouldn't have done it—I should have said, 'Well this is too hard, I shouldn't do this.' But it really is a question of character and sense of self and who you are, and a trusting of your own instincts, and I think Roy has that in spades."

Offering a Strong Shoulder

Veteran producer Ted Snowdon echoes Dietz's view of Gabay. Snowdon first met Gabay twelve years ago after Gabay approached him to produce a one-man show, *Virgin and Other Myths* by a college friend of his, Colin Martin. Snowdon produced the show at Primary Stages, an off-Broadway venue, with Gabay coming on board as an associate producer and general manager. Since then, Snowdon has used Gabay as a general manager for a number of shows. He's also used him as a sounding board for ideas for shows.

During the 2005–06 season, Gabay worked as a general manager for the ill-fated Broadway production *Souvenir,* about the life of the 1930s Manhattan socialite Florence Foster Jenkins, who thought she was a great coloratura soprano when she was anything but, a project that Snowdon pro-duced (and whose failure to find an audience still gnaws at him). Gabay was a pillar of support Snowdon greatly depended upon—and still does.

"He had a great deal to say on the day-to-day operations, always remind-ing me of the bills and situation—the practical side of producing, which some of us idealists don't want to think about too much. So he's very good that way. He's a no-nonsense kind of person who doesn't have fancy office space.... There was a lot of terrible backlash with *Souvenir* after it closed. He stuck by me all the way. He does a great job [as a GM] and everything operates smoothly. However, nothing goes smoothly unless you're selling at the box office," says Snowdon, emitting a protracted sigh. "He's one of the younger persons who's a dying breed because he believes that some things can still find an audience and are of good to the world. I don't know, because we keep taking a beating, so I don't know how long it's going to go on."

(Ironically, Snowdon is enjoying a tremendous upswing with his long-standing career right now. A coproducer of *The Little Dog Laughed*, he is also on the team behind *Spring Awakening*, a rock musical adaptation of the Franz Wedekind play about hormonal adolescents in Germany in the 1890s; the production not only elicited gushing reviews from critics, but scored eight Tony Awards, including Best Musical.)

Snowdon got involved with *The Little Dog Laughed* after Gabay phoned him to tell him he secured the rights and wanted him to come on board.

Having seen the show in its off-Broadway incarnation at Second Stage, Snowdon agreed.

"He's not only pragmatic, he's democratic. Roy likes to spread the effort around. He's not really ego-driven or into taking all the credit himself. He's kind of self-effacing in that way. So it was about roping in or bringing in other partners to make it a reality while he did all the dirty work, like fighting with the agents to make it happen, which he's very good at."

Gabay feels that *Little Dog* marks yet another decisive moment in his career because it's an original play—and an American comedy, at that—which is becoming endangered species on Broadway.

"All the time we hear from people, 'God, it's so nice to be entertained. We haven't been in so long.' You feel smart after seeing it, but it's not over your head. I mean, as much as *The History Boys* (Alan Bennett's play that won the 2006 Tony Award for Best Play) was great, a lot of people just didn't get it." (Sadly for Gabay and Dietz, *The Little Dog Laughed* closed on February 19, 2007, playing only for 112 performances. But all was not lost. It did have one triumphant aftereffect: Julie White won the Tony for Best Actress in a Play.)

Regrettably, notes Gabay, a large segment of the Broadway audience is comprised of non-English speakers, which make plays a very hard sell. Many would rather see *Hairspray*, where at least they can enjoy the singing and choreography, even if they don't quite understand the book.

Keeping Expenses Under Control

For Gabay, the most challenging aspect of being a producer on the present-day Broadway landscape is not raising the money, but keeping the show within budget at a time when overall expenses for salaries, equipment, and rents are spiraling out of control. This has become a serious quandary for most contemporary producers. And it's one that doesn't seem to be going away in the near future. It's especially difficult when you're dealing with a nonmusical.

"There's no bad guy in this equation. It's just that there are a lot of costs that are going up, and unfortunately audiences for plays are not going up proportionally. We're making it so impossible for a play to recoup." On the other hand, a producer should be able to swallow his or her pride and know when to close a show that's clearly doomed at the box office. Gabay believes this is a quality that every good producer should possess.

"I honestly think that's one of the most important things a producer should be able to do. Like when Daryl Roth closed *Mambo Kings* before it came to New York [the show, an adaptation of the 1992 movie starring Antonio Banderas, was supposed to arrive on Broadway in 2005 but never made it due to disastrous out-of-town notices], or being in New York and realizing you're not going to make it and closing it. There's so much pressure on you as a producer to keep it open, to keep working on it, to keep bringing it in, to keep spending money on the creative team. They're great, but they don't understand the great fiscal responsibilities we have, and there's so much pressure from them and their agents to keep it going that I think any of us who can stand up to that and say, 'You know, it's not going to work'—I admire that greatly in people."

Right now, Gabay is working on transferring *Rejoice*, an original musical that performed at the National Black Arts Festival in Atlanta in July 2006, to Broadway in the near future. The work, which centers on the gospel music of Thomas A. Dorsey, features a book by Cheryl West and music by Kenny Leon.

His advice to budding producers? "Find writers and directors you're passionate about. That's the best connection to producing. If you find a good show, if you find a good writer, a good director, if you find a good project, you'll get the money. I think people try to go from the money first, and I don't think that ever works because the money is the money, but what are you doing with it? It's all about the material."

Career Highlights

- Started off as an intern in producer Elizabeth McCann's office
- Was a general manager before he was a producer; he still works as a general manager from time to time
- First show he worked on as a general manager was the off-Broadway production of *Three Tall Women*, which ran from April 13, 1994 to August 26, 1995 at the Promenade Theatre; Gabay, initially worked on the show as a company manager and later replaced the general manager after he left
- First show he produced was the off-Broadway production of *How I Learned to Drive*, which ran from May 6, 1997 to April 19, 1998, at the Century Center for the Performing Arts
- Coproduced with Elizabeth McCann the Broadway transfer (December 14, 1997 to August 30, 1998) of *A View from the Bridge*; this was the first Broadway show he worked on as a producer
- Produced the highly acclaimed Broadway transfer (March 4, 2002-February 16, 2003) of *Metamorphoses*
- Produced the Tony-nominated *The Little Dog Laughed*, which had a brief Broadway run, from November 13, 2006 to February 18, 2007

Bibliography

Bloom, Ken. *Broadway: An Encyclopedic Guide to the History, People and Places of Times Square.* New York: Facts on File, 1991.

Epstein, Helen. *Joe Papp: An American Life.* Boston: Little Brown & Company Ltd., 1994.

Hartmann, Louis. *Theatre Lighting (A Manual of the Stage Switchboard).* New York: D. Appleton and Company, 1930.

Higham, Charles. *Ziegfeld.* Chicago: Henry Regnery Company, 1972.

Kenrick, John. *Ziegfeld 101/Florenz Ziegfeld: A Biography, 2002–2004. www.musicals101.com/ziegfeld.htm,* accessed October 2006.

Kissel, Howard. *David Merrick: The Abominable Showman: An Unauthorized Biography.* New York: Applause Books, 1993.

Little, Stuart W. *Enter Joseph Papp: In Search of a New American Theater.* New York: Coward, McCann & Geoghegan, Inc., 1974.

Little, Stuart W. *Off Broadway: The Prophetic Theater.* New York: Coward, McCann & Geoghegan, Inc., 1972.

Marker, Lisa-Lone. *David Belasco: Naturalism in the Theatre.* Princeton, N.J.: Princeton University Press, 1975.

Appendix

Noteworthy Training Programs

For those wishing to undertake a crash course in producing, or an in-depth exploration, CTI's various programs may be the ticket.

The Commercial Theater Institute

The Commercial Theater Institute's annual producing seminars have two different types of programs: the three-day program, which is held the last weekend in April; and the fourteen-week program, held from early February through early May. Staffed by experienced professionals who run the gamut from working producers and attorneys to press agents and general managers, CTI offers classes on the following hot-button topics to aspiring producers and investors: legal aspects of commercial producing; developing investors; case studies of Broadway and off-Broadway productions; for-profit/not-for-profit relationships; producing for the road; marketing the commercial theater; and budget outline and analysis.

For additional information, or to register, please contact: Alan Cohen, Director of Communications, League of American Theatres and Producers, (212) 703-0225, ACohen@Broadway.org, or visit *www.commercialtheaterinstitute.com*.

Colleges/Universities

Though there are no BFAs or MFAs presently offered in producing, there are many top-notch universities that provide degree programs in theater management, of which producing is an important component. Following is a list of programs for your edification and review:

University of Alabama and Alabama
Shakespeare Festival/MFA
www.asf.net

Arizona State University/BA
www.asu.edu

Auburn University/BFA
www.auburn.edu

Baldwin-Wallace College/BA
www.bw.edu

Boston College/BA
www.bc.edu

Brenau University/BFA
www.brenau.edu

Brooklyn College/MFA
www.brooklyn.cuny.edu

Butler University/BS
www.butler.edu

California Institute of the Arts/BFA
and MFA
www.calarts.edu

California State University, Long
Beach/MFA
www.csulb.edu

Carnegie Mellon University/BFA
and MFA
www.cmu.edu/cfa/drama

Catawba College/BS
www.catawba.edu

Central Washington University/BA
www.cwu.edu

College of Santa Fe/BFA
www.csf.edu

Columbia University/MFA
www.columbia.edu/cu/arts/theatre

Culver Stockton College/BA and
BFA
www.culver.edu

Eastern Michigan State University/
BA and BS
www.emich.edu/cta

Emerson College/BA, BFA and BS
www.emerson.edu

Florida Atlantic University/MFA
www.fau.edu

Florida International University/BA
www.fiu.edu

Graceland College/BA
www.graceland.edu

Howard University/BFA
www.howard.edu

Illinois State University/MBA
www.ilstu.edu

Indiana State University/BA, BS,
MA, and MS
www.indstate.edu

Indiana University/MA
www.fa.indiana.edu/~thtr

Ithaca College/BS
www.ithaca.edu/theatre

Longwood University/BFA
www.longwood.edu

Loyola University New Orleans/BA
www.loyno.edu

Mary Baldwin College/BA
www.mbc.edu

North Carolina Agricultural and
Technical State University/BFA
www.ncat.edu

Northern Kentucky University/BFA
www.nku.edu

Ohio Wesleyan University/BA
www.owu.edu

Pace University/BFA
www.pace.edu

Rutgers University, New Brunswick/
BFA
www.rutgers.edu

St. Edwards University/BA
www.stedwards.edu

Theatre at Point Park University/BA
and BFA
www.pointpark.edu

Theatre School at DePaul
University/BFA
http://theatreschool.depaul.edu/

University of Alabama, Tuscaloosa/
MFA
www.as.ua.edu/theatre

University of Evansville/BS
www.evansville.edu

University of Illinois at Urbana-
Champaign/BFA and MFA
www.uiuc.edu

University of Miami/BFA
www.miami.edu/tha

University of Portland/BS
www.up.edu

University of Rhode Island/BFA
www.uri.edu

University of Texas-Pan American/BA
www.panam.edu

University of
Wisconsin - Whitewater/BFA
www.uww.edu

Virginia Tech/MFA
www.vt.edu

Viterbo College/BFA
www.viterbo.edu

Wagner College/BA
www.wagner.edu

Wayne State University/MFA
www.wayne.edu

Western Michigan University/BA
www.wmich.edu

Yale University School of Drama/MFA
www.yale.edu/drama

Books

To read more about the intricacies and legalities of producing, here are some worthy volumes:

Faber, Donald. *From Option to Opening: A Guide to Producing Plays Off Broadway.* New York: Limelight Editions, 2005.

Faber, Donald. *Producing Theatre: A Comprehensive and Legal Business Guide.* New York: Limelight Editions, 2006.

Gardyne, John. *Producing Musicals: A Practical Guide.* U.K: Crowood Press, Limited, 2004.

Grippo, Charles. *The Stage Producer's Business and Legal Guide.* New York: Allworth Press, 2002.

Hodges, Frederic B. and Ben Hodges, eds. *The Commercial Theater Institute's Guide to Producing Plays and Musicals.* New York: Applause Theatre & Cinema Books, 2006.

Organizations

Actors' Equity Association
National Headquarters
165 West 46th Street
New York, NY 10036
212-869-8530
www.actorsequity.org
Union for professional theater actors and stage managers who work in legit theater.

American Theatre Wing
570 Seventh Avenue
Suite 501
New York, NY 10018
212-765-0606
www.americantheatrewing.org
Creator and a producer of the annual Tony Awards, which recognize excellence in the Broadway theater, the American Theatre Wing is a not-for-profit organization that promotes educational outreach and activities relating to theater for students and audiences.

Society of Stage Directors and Choregraphers
1501 Broadway, Suite 1701
New York, NY 10036-5653
toll-free: (800) 541-5204
in NYC: (212) 391-1070
www.ssdc.org
An independent labor union that represents professional theater directors
and choreographers throughout the United States and abroad.

The League of American Theatres and Producers
226 West 47th St.
New York, NY 10036
212-703-0225
Founded in 1930, this organization is comprised of 600 plus members, many
of whom are theater owners and operators, producers, presenters, general
managers and industry suppliers in North America.

The Dramatists Guild of America
1501 Broadway
Suite 701
New York, NY 10036
212-398-9366
www.dramatistsguild.com
This association, more than eighty years old, boasts over six thousand
members worldwide, including playwrights, lyricists, and composers.

Publications

Hollywood Reporter
5055 Wilshire Boulevard
Los Angeles, CA 90036
213-525-2000
www.hollywoodreporter.com
An industry trade weekly that reports breaking news in legit theater, as well as
top Broadway grossers of that week.

Theatrical Index
888 Eighth Avenue
New York, NY 10019
212-585-6342

Contains information on what's running on Broadway, off-Broadway, and on national tours, including details on producers, general managers, press agents, and opening dates. Also included is information on what's coming to Broadway and off-Broadway.

Variety/Daily Variety
5700 Wilshire Boulevard
Suite 120
Los Angeles, CA 90036-5804
323-965-4476
www.variety.com
Another industry trade that's also a bible for entertainment professionals.

INDEX

Books from Allworth Press

Allworth Press is an imprint of Allworth Communications, Inc. Selected titles are listed below.

Making It on Broadway: Actors' Tales of Climbing to the Top
by David Wiener and Jodie Langel (6 × 9, 288 pages, paperback, $19.95)

Letters from Backstage: The Adventures of a Touring Stage Actor
by Michael Kostroff (6 × 9, 224 pages, paperback, $16.95)

Running Theaters: Best Practices for Leaders and Managers
by Duncan M. Webb (6 × 9, 256 pages, paperback, $19.95)

Building the Successful Theater Company
by Lisa Mulcahy (6 × 9, 240 pages, paperback, $19.95)

The Stage Producer's Business and Legal Guide
by Charles Grippo (6 × 9, 256 pages, paperback, $19.95)

Booking Performance Tours: Marketing and Acquiring Live Arts and Entertainment
by Tony Micocci (6 × 9, 304 pages, paperback, $24.95)

How to Improvise a Full-Length Play: The Art of Spontaneous Theater
by Kenn Adams (5 1/2 × 8 1/2, 176 pages, paperback, $16.95)

Singing in Musical Theatre: The Training of Singers and Actors
by Joan Melton (6 × 9, 240 pages, paperback, $19.95)

Acting the Song: Performance Skills for the Musical Theater
by Tracey Moore with Allison Bergman (6 × 9, 304 pages, paperback, $24.95)

Acting Teachers of America
by Ronald Rand and Luigi Scorcia (6 × 9, 288 pages, 75 b&w illustrations, $19.95)

Actor Training the Laban Way: An Integrated Approach to Voice, Speech, and Movement
by Barbara Adrian (7 3/8 × 9 1/4, 256 pages, paperback, $24.95)

Acting: Advanced Techniques for the Actor, Director, and Teacher
by Terry Schreiber (6 × 9, 256 pages, paperback, $19.95)

To request a free catalog or order books by credit card, call 1-800-491-2808. To see our complete catalog on the World Wide Web, or to order online for a 20 percent discount, you can find us at **www.allworth.com.**